EVANGELISM
for TEEN-AGERS

HOWARD W. ELLIS

EVANGELISM
for TEEN-AGERS

for a new day

ABINGDON PRESS
Nashville   New York

EVANGELISM FOR TEEN-AGERS

Library of Congress Catalog Card Number: 66-20457

SET UP, PRINTED, AND BOUND BY THE
PARTHENON PRESS, AT NASHVILLE,
TENNESSEE, UNITED STATES OF AMERICA

Preface to the Revised Edition

I am grateful for this opportunity to revise and update *Evangelism for Teen-Agers* at this time. The editors and publishers have given me a free hand and unqualified support in the process.

When I began rewriting I did not envision that so many changes would need to be made—nor so few. The basic assumptions about the need for action projects in youth-to-youth evangelism that prompted this movement in the life of the church in the first place have not changed. But the theory and practice of the youth ministry in our Protestant churches are in the throes of radical revision. *Evangelism for Teen-Agers* can, we believe, continue to be a timely resource because of the validity of our basic assumption, namely: *that committed Christian young people are the best instruments to extend the Christian fellowship to other young people.* This has been our guide to action.

There are some obvious changes of emphasis emerging. Youth are seen not as the church of the future but as the church in action. There is keener awareness of the alienation of many young people from the church. The sickness and evangelism failure of the youth fellowship in the local church is faced frankly. The greatest need of the church is not to recruit more of the same kind of Christians we've got now. The need is for renewal and growth.

Fortunately a gospel of relationship is beginning to emerge that gives promise of transforming the darkest of human experiences and attitudes and of bringing renewal to a broken and fragmented church. Wherever

5

the gospel-in-relationship is one of openness to others and to God, growth comes—spiritual growth and numerical growth. Both are essential to a redemptive fellowship.

Again, my gratitude to the young people and adults who work with youth all across this continent and abroad, who are the real authors of this work. I am grateful for my co-workers everywhere who have made many valuable contributions. And while I have this chance, may I rededicate this little book to my wife, Susanna, my own two young people, Patsy Sue and Mary Lou, and to my former secretary, Miss Ada McKinley. And may I affectionately add to this preface my best wishes to my good friend and fellow worker, Bill Peckham, who now begins where this book comes out with a wholehearted involvement with teens in their world.

HOWARD W. ELLIS
Nashville, Tennessee
January, 1966

Contents

Contents

Remember also your Creator in the days of your youth.

—Eccl. 12:1

1

HERE COMES TOMORROW—TODAY

The ever-present danger of your life is that, having been born into Christianity, Christianity may never get born in you.

—Hazen G. Werner

If you're a teen-ager, you can take some comfort in this: never before in history has our nation turned the searchlight so intensely on our younger generation. Educators study you. Your parents worry over you. People like me write books about you. You may have the distinction of being the most analyzed but least understood youth in history. You were born in the aftermath of war. You've grown up in an age of constant turmoil. You're bigger, you're smarter, and you're better fed than many of the other kids in our mighty neighborhood. You're full of zany antics, wonderful good humor, and plain common sense. Naturally, you don't like to hear people say: "irresponsible teen-agers," "juvenile delinquents," "rock-and-roll swooners," or "teen gangs." Yet that's part of the picture.

9

The Spotlight Is on Youth

Yes, teen-agers are on the spot in public opinion. You know that. For many critical commentators, our teens seem to present more problems than promise.

The newspapers and magazines are giving us plenty of evidence that we've got a teen-ager problem. Just take a few of the headlines and the stories behind them:

"17 JUVENILES NABBED FOR BRUTALITY." A gang of toughs are sentenced by a juvenile judge for unprovoked attacks on innocent high-school students.

"HELD IN SCHOOL RAIDS." Unidentified young vandals launch a series of night raids on the schools of a large city. They break furniture, spill ink on books, deface desks, smash windows. Nearly half the windows in the school are broken. Damage is estimated at $1,000.

"KILL FOR THRILLS, WHIP GIRLS," another headline screams.

And still another front-page headline says: "TEEN KILLERS POSE MYSTERY. WHY DID THEY DO IT? POLICE WONDER." The story: A baffled district attorney asks for ten days' adjournment of court to study the habits and home lives of four Brooklyn teen-agers. The four boys find a young man on a park bench. They beat him, burn his feet, torture him, push him, dazed, to the East River and toss him in. Police find his body several days later.

The headlines and stories, of course, are only a symptom of a deeper problem. Any way you look at the situation, it is big and puzzling. Even the experts are stumped.

In his book *1,000,000 Delinquents* Benjamin Fine points out that we have more than one million juvenile delinquents a year. He goes on to say: "All the evidence suggests that we are on a tragic upswing. Teen-age law breakers are becoming more numerous and their crimes more serious."

Parents have a right to ask: "What is the church doing about our youth?"

What about these young people outside the church? They're not all delinquents. Not by a long shot! Less than 5 percent of them get in trouble serious enough to be picked up by the police.

It's hard to get reliable figures on this crowd. But take the figures of organized religion in America. A few years ago the churches reported 7,290,000 young people aged 12 to 23 enrolled in religious activities. At the time these figures were put out, the youth population stood at 26,618,240. This leaves a staggering total of 19,328,000 youth unaccounted for! Nearly twenty million youth A.W.O.L., if these startling figures may be trusted.

This means that three out of four young people are outside the church —anybody's church.

Suppose we stand on the front steps of your church—somewhere inside U.S.A. Watch them march by.

Begin in January. Start the line of march in New York City—Broadway. Give them a big send-off. Here they come! Marching. Five in a row—five seconds apart—marching.

Tramp—tramp—five in a row—five seconds apart—in a line of march that stretches out all the way across the continent, then back again to St. Louis. Four thousand miles of them!

These are the unchurched youth of America!

Let's just look at one city for a moment. Take Pittsburgh. One of our leading churchmen says: "In any single year in Pittsburgh, we have more kids picked up by the police and brought into court than we have enrolled in all of the Methodist youth fellowships of Greater Pittsburgh!"

Meeting the Teen-Age Invasion

The Christian Century dramatically underlines the problem that this rising tide of teen-agers present to society and to the church:

Three million seven hundred thousand United States teen-agers celebrated their 17th birthday in 1964, one million more than in 1963. . . . At the end of the coming decade the 17-year-old population will reach the 4 million level. The family and social problems created by this rising teen-age population threaten to become increasingly massive and complex. By 1974 high school enrollment will swell from this year's 12.7 million to 16.3 million. . . .

One-fourth of all 17-year-olds have already become "dropouts" and are flooding a labor market which increasingly demands a high school diploma as the minimum educational requirement. . . . Given these conditions it is not surprising that teen-age crime and juvenile delinquency soar. In the post-war years the proportion as well as the actual number of juvenile arrests has increased sharply and both continue to increase. Over one-third of the males who married in their 17th year or before and about one-fifth of the females are now divorced or separated. The seemingly easy way out of some problems catapults adolescents into other problems which are even more serious. . . . Despite the success of most adolescents in handling the problems successfully themselves, the number not so successful or so fortunate presents a major crisis which cannot be resolved until it is treated as a major crisis demanding the concerted action of all institutions concerned about the problems of youth. No matter how efficiently any one of the institutions does its duty to teen-agers, the total problem, an accelerating force, will outrun the unilateral solutions offered by churches, schools, social agencies and government. We have in our swelling teen-age population both a threat and an opportunity. Today and not later we must act together to ensure that the teen-age invasion becomes a blessing rather than a curse.[1]

What Young People Are Saying

This is, for the teen-ager, a difficult society to cope with. They are thrust into the adult world so fast that they are almost middle-aged in their teens. Parents are as puzzled by their offspring's precocious ways as the children are. For parents and children, this is a generation that is pushed so hard that adolescence is disappearing into adulthood—"too old too soon." Edgar Z. Friedenberg calls this generation of youngsters *The Vanishing Adolescent*.[2] And with good reason. Listen to what they are saying—this generation which the Gallup poll calls "The Cool Generation":

Education is often the most neglected extracurricular activity: *"It's not the grades that matter, but whether you're popular."*

Our typical youth will settle for low success rather than risk high failure. He has little spirit of adventure. He wants *"a little ranch house, an inexpensive new car, a job with a large company, a chance to watch TV each evening after the smiling children are asleep in bed."*

He may be highly religious, yet wink at honesty: *"Any normal person will cheat in school. It's up to the teacher to put a stop to it."*

He feels that nothing he does will make any difference: *"You know, there are no individuals any more. There are no more Lindberghs flying the ocean alone, or real men with real names and real identities exploring the frozen north. It's all done by teamwork and helicopters and submarines backstopped by a thousand scientists and technicians. Even the astronauts are not people; they're a team."*

He is not shocked by anything: *"How can we be indignant, especially after knowing what we do about World War II and humanity?"*

Young people are confused. They live in a world that is hard to understand: *"I don't know. For eight years now—for almost half our lives—we've been told that everything is peachy fine. Now we know it's not. Americans have been treated like children and denied the harsh truths. Now we're told to act, but we don't know what to do. I'm confused."*

They are not altogether blissfully ignorant of the alternatives to freedom and democracy: *"I don't know enough about Communism to talk about it. Everybody says it's bad, but we're never told what it is. I think the people who want us to be better teen-agers should tell us what Communism is."*

It is not easy to be secure in a world of contradiction, disillusion, and controversy, but our youth seem to have succeeded. In doing so, many of them have turned inward, speaking only to themselves, living portions of their lives without meaning or responsibility. The young person is engulfed in privatism. His only human values are those in his own immediate life. His greatest concerns include a package of personal irritants he calls "the future." He is concerned about *"job-finding, wife-hunting and nest-making."*

"I'm just dying to travel. But I've gotta go first class, of course."

The young person knows only the horizontal society, and even this society he doesn't know well.

His greatest fears are immediate and personal. He is afraid of making a fool of himself in public or *"not being respected." "Being laughed at is very hurtful."*

American youth correctly blame others for the problems facing them and incorrectly say that others will solve the problems for them.

A young Kirkland Air Force Base pilot prepares to wage nuclear war in space six days a week; on Sunday he turns to God. He says: *"I know that my work can contribute to great violence, but it can be used for good as well as horrible destruction. Man will decide to use it as he sees fit."* Here is our chronic contemporary buck-passing. We divorce ourselves from mankind, saying, "Man will decide," as though we are not a part of man.

Contemporary youth as a whole seem to be religious, yet quite critical of the church as an institution. The most frequent complaints are that the church fails to explain itself and its precepts, that it fails to stress its true meaning fervently enough, that it is not reaching the people, and that sermons are too vague and muddy. This comment is typical: *"[Religion is] getting to be a vending machine. You put in a nickel and you get a reward. It doesn't lead the people; it merely reflects their values."*

This is an attempt to draw a miniature group portrait of the puzzling youth of today that the *Saturday Evening Post*'s Gallup Poll survey calls "the cool generation." [3] Any composite portrait is of course always likely to be distorted, one-sided, or incomplete. But adolescents seem to be asking some questions for which the Christian community needs to help them find some answers.

Youth want to know:

Who am I? Are there any dependable answers to what a human being is?

What working models of selfhood can I trust?

What will support my desirable self as I see myself?

How can I be the person I would like to be?

What expectations can I reasonably hold for my life?

Where can I find a model for the manhood into which I am moving?

Underneath all of these questions and probing is an agonizing search for meaning. Young people are searching for identity, for intimacy, for some ultimate meaning to which they can commit their lives.

Youth Are Laymen—Now

This book shows how young people, with their adult leaders, are responsible for the church's ministry to youth and not just "the church of tomorrow." Tomorrow is here now. Youth are in lively dialogue with the gospel and the world—now. Christian youth are already full partners in the mission of the church—"We answer God's call to be the Christian community." The call is an evangelistic call. For it is as we do the work of evangelism and try to put our faith into action through dialogue and interpersonal relations that we discover the mission of the church.

This mission begun by Jesus Christ, shared with the Twelve, continued in his church, is carried out as all Christians fulfill their discipleship in the world. The church exists in the world. But the church is no place for evangelism. Evangelism—the extension of the Christian fellowship into the world—must be done in the world. The world of the high school young person is the high school community.

There is growing evidence that youth and adults who are responsible for the youth evangelism movement are making some significant efforts to penetrate this high school community with the gospel.

If we assume that our task in youth evangelism is to get youth deeply involved in the youth fellowship in order to train youth for the future church of tomorrow, we will have missed the most important fact about the church's ministry with youth, namely: *Youth are laity, responsible along with adults for the church's total ministry.*[4]

Youth and adults share the same baptism; assume the same membership vows; share the one mission of the church. Laity are God's people participating in the mission to the world: to make Jesus Christ known, loved, trusted, obeyed. Young people share this responsibility, too. Responsible participation in the Christian community calls for every Christian's prayers, presence, gifts, and service.

The role of the Christian in society demands faithfulness and obedience from young people *now* as well as later. While they are growing in their faith, youth are involved in their high school community; their fraternity or sorority; their part-time job; their family; sports; dates; their own peculiar culture of status symbols, myths, and meaning. This is their world in which youth must be the church. Their future is here—now.

To regard youth as laity broadens their responsibilities in the church as full partners with adults in study together, in worship, witness, outreach, and service.

The best way to keep the youth you get is to regard them as members-in-mission, rather than members-in-preparation.

Where youth are searching for identity, Christ offers Christian commitment.

Where youth are searching for intimacy, Christ offers Christian community.

Where youth are searching for ultimate meaning, Christ offers Christian commission.

Teen-agers involved in evangelism is the story of this search and this offer.

Do not be conformed to this world but be transformed by the renewal of our mind, that you may prove what is the will of God, what is good and acceptable and perfect.

—Rom. 12:2

2

THE STRUGGLE FOR RENEWAL

The place of the community of Christ is at the perilous moving edges of change where Christ is offering to men a participation in the life of the new humanity.

—Colin W. Williams

The church of Jesus Christ is living today in one of those agonizing yet promising times of radical reappraisal and renewal. You see signs of this struggle for renewal everywhere—and it *is* a struggle, and it *is* painful. These swift and radical changes are the growing pains of adolescence, when a person finds that he is too young to be an adult and too old to be a young person.

It is certain that our youth ministry stands on the threshold of great changes. Let it be said loudly and clearly that this renewal is not to be feared but welcomed. Here the ever reforming church touches the life of youth. The crisis within Christendom finds the youth ministry more open to change than other aspects of the life and work of the church. The church's youth program is serving as a laboratory of ex-

17

perimentation and exploration and testing of new forms of ministry. Here in the youth program is an exciting preview of coming attractions.

When will the church of the future be born? We are in it now. Every church today has its share of experiments looking ahead to the twenty-first century. The unconventional is becoming commonplace. The reformers of today, among whom are so many adult workers with youth, believe in total renewal because, in the words of Dr. Harvey Cox of Harvard Divinity School, "the existing pattern of the church is no longer in touch with real life."

This chapter is an attempt to involve you and, through you, your church in some of the critical issues in evangelism facing youth today throughout the world. This book does not claim to embrace all that is involved in the shaking of the foundations of the old evangelistic structure and the building of the new. I can only share what seem to me the significant problems and creative opportunities facing Christians, youth and adults, as together we strive to see the road ahead. Conventional wisdom is clearly not enough to communicate the Christian gospel to the youth in contemporary culture. We need the insights of tomorrow for today.

Traditional adolescence is on its way out—indeed, it has gone. For the first time in the history of the planet, it is impossible for a father to convey to his son with any degree of clarity the kind of world situation he may expect as an adult. In *West Side Story* one of the gang members confronts Officer Krupke, who is telling the boys how things were when he was their age. The boy says: "Officer Krupke, you never were our age!"

There is a growing conviction among those responsible for shaping the church's ministry to youth that a completely new strategy is now called for. Obviously, there are differences between youth and adults in the church. But the difference is in age, not in responsibility. Youth and adults are confronting the same rapid changes in human society, the depersonalization and fragmentation of the individual. In the light of the vast changes and the swift pace of change, there is little wonder that both youth and adults are bewildered. It is not change itself, but the accelerated pace of change that is so difficult to cope with.

Never before have we been so dependent upon the decisions of others that we never hear nor see. The city where more than 75 percent of the young people and their parents now live is an impersonal place. The city is filled with rootless, fragmented, communityless, lonely people. No longer can a person say, "I belong." We have witnessed the phenomenon of people standing passively aside in the streets, watching as defenseless girls were stabbed to death before their eyes or women suffered the pangs of childbirth or hopeless men threatened to commit suicide. Nobody cared. The riots in our city streets reveal that vast numbers of persons are totally disenchanted with the status quo and are caught in a web of hopelessness and despair. The mounting numbers of dropouts from high school, the chronic unemployment of the teen-agers coming into the labor force, the alienation of multitudes of socially deviant youth demands revolutionary reassessment of our youth situation in society and in the churches.

Despite such changes, the youth program of our Protestant churches has changed little in its format and structure in this century. The minimum program in the average local church consists of an hour of study on Sunday morning under the guidance of a teacher and an hour on Sunday evening under the direction of youth officers and adult counselors. Christian education is conducted by lay persons who give their time voluntarily. For the most part, all that is required of them is that they are willing to stand up and try. The dedication and commitment of these people are not questioned. Their motives are high, their hopes commendable. But there is a communication breakdown that arises from the demands of the situation. The evidence is overwhelming that neither the facts of the gospel nor the power of the gospel is getting through to teen-agers.

Evangelism failure in the youth work of the Protestant churches is a painful fact. A thoughtful appraisal of the limited success of the church in communicating the Christian gospel to youth in contemporary culture compels us to ask the question: How does one communicate the Christian gospel to youth in contemporary culture?

Workers with youth throughout the church share a growing conviction that the pattern of youth work in the local church has long been due for a drastic overhauling. It is true that the camps and conferences and institutes and retreats beyond the local church are usually well planned and often thrilling. But the youth work of our churches is sick at the local level.

What is the reason for this critical evangelism failure in the local church and the much higher performance in quality of program and communication of the Christian gospel outside the local church in retreats, camps, and conferences? If young people come to believe that God is to be found only in camp settings among mountains, lakes, or woods, we may convey an Old Testament view of a God who is to be found only in far-off holy places, rather than in the ordinary ventures of life.

The impact of these special experiences lies largely in the fact that in these settings, young people often discover what it means "to be," "to belong," and "to do." In the unapologetic call to commitment of the camp, young people learn what it means *to be* a Christian. In the intimate community that develops during a camp, young people experience what it means *to belong* to the Christian community. In the setting where the meaning of Christian vocation is sharpened and young people discover a commission *to do* something with their lives, the Great Commission becomes a reality—an "I–thou" encounter with the missionary movement of the Christian faith.

The efforts in renewal of the church that are related to the youth ministry all focus on these three essentials of our faith: commitment, community, and commission. The depth Bible study groups are efforts to help young people find the biblical basis for what it means *to be* a Christian. The renewal groups in the church are struggling to achieve a sense of the New Testament *koinonia* or fellowship—what it means *to belong* to the Christian community. The evangelistic ventures in Christian Witness Missions, Impact! and the many experimental ministries including those we shall preview in the next chapter, "Toward a Vital Youth Fellowship," are efforts to achieve a sense of what it means *to do* something about the Christian's commission to witness to the power of the gospel in the world.

This struggle for renewal may be seen in clearer perspective if we can focus on some of the ways youth groups are going about their work in renewal groups and depth Bible study.

Guidelines for the Renewal Groups

1. *The groups are small.* Usually twelve persons constitute a group. When groups are larger they subdivide. Free interchange and individual expression is encouraged.

2. *The group accepts some basic disciplines.* These rules to live by may include the following disciplines:

—Daily devotions alone with the family.

—Regular worship in the small group and in weekly public worship.

—Sacrificial giving. A definite portion of money and time given regularly to the Christian cause.

—Disciplined study. A development of intellectual integrity by a careful study of the Christian faith.

—Unapologetic witness in daily life, in words, in work.

3. *The group sets its meeting places, times, and style of meetings.* A house meeting is best. A commitment to attend ten or twelve consecutive meetings is a prerequisite to get a group going. An agreed "cut-off" period allows the group to voluntarily continue, divide, or enlist others.

4. *The group deals with the gospel in relationship.* The key word is "encounter." Whatever form the group life takes, it is necessary to deal both with facts and feelings—with a study of the facts of the gospel and how we feel about them, really. Masks come off as persons learn it is all right to be themselves.

5. *The group accepts responsibility for evangelistic mission in the world.* Intercessory prayer becomes a possibility when it is accompanied

by meaningful action. There are many areas of service open to young people. Some possibilities: helping in the "head start" program for pre-school children, play ground supervision, "candy-stripers" in the hospital, helpers in homes for crippled and handicapped children, visiting the aged and shut-ins. The dangers of becoming ingrown are avoided when from the beginning the members accept responsibility for mission to the outsider, the lonely, and the alienated.

In the army, basic training comes in the small group. So the soldiers for Christ learn their "basics" in these small face-to-face groups. This is new and yet it is not new. It started in Galilee. The early Christians met in house churches. The church recovered its mission in England when John Wesley rediscovered new life for the church in the small class meetings where Christians opened up their lives to one another and to God.

The disciplined group offers such a promising venture for renewal of the youth ministry that small core groups of youth and adults constitute a major thrust into the twenty-first century pattern of church life. Today the growing experience and accumulated resources for small renewal groups give evidence that this recovery of discipleship in small groups throughout Christendom is sparking a new encounter with the Living Word as a dynamic relationship between God, man, Christ, and the church.[1]

How to Do Depth Bible Study

Bible study is coming alive for many young people through paraphrasing or depth Bible study. This is a way of helping to make the ancient words live in a new way through making your own personal translation of the Bible—the Bible according to you. Here are the guidelines for this style of Bible study:

1. *See what you can make of the biblical passage.* The ground rule for doing this is: Put this verse in your own words—not using any of the major words which the Bible uses. This rule is most important—for if you really grasp what is being said, you can say it in other words. This ground rule particularly applies to such words as "God," "Christ,"

"sin," "love." Try to translate the passage into the daily, earthy language with which you and yours feel, think, imagine, plan. Write the verse as you would say it. Say it directly and with force.

Sometimes you will enjoy trying to put the verse in the thought and action world of a particular group of people—say psychiatrists, teachers, your parents, the mailman, the delinquent-prone adolescent or the disinherited intelligentsia. For you should be able to speak of the heart of religion in the direct and simple language which will communicate to all kinds of people, not just to the academic mind. In general your translation should not be much longer than the original verse.

2. *Jot down what this verse—and your translation of it—awakens in you.* Let what you have written "see, feel, think, reconstruct" for you. Explore beyond the limits of what you already are, be original. Just one significant thing, allowed to grow and mature, is more important than making a long list. The following questions may help: If I took the Bible verse seriously,

Would I see some persons and situations any differently than I now do?

Would I feel about myself and my actions in a fresh way? What would I care for, be concerned about? Is there here a live option for action? A realistic choice here offered? What would I (and others) do differently?

Keep it existential; don't make out suggestions that would be good for other people to feel and do! The Bible is the Word of God for you only when it speaks to you.

3. *Meet together as a group.* First take time to understand and nurture (help it grow) each person's translation. Don't just have him read it and then hurry on to the next person, but savor the interesting uniqueness of it, find out more of what he was trying to say by the phrases and key words that he used. He really had something in his mind, and it's a lot more than he could say in a sentence.

4. *Share the reflections you jotted down.* What if I took this Bible verse seriously? What has been awakened in me? It could be rebellion against it. Let this period be "one freedom talking to another

freedom," a give and take as the spirit moves. There will probably emerge some main issues or convictions that your group will want to concentrate on. Go after these with real fierceness; life is too short to be filled with clichés and pleasantries.[2]

A New Pattern for Old First

The great struggle in work with youth is to find more time and to achieve greater depth in local church program. Since "Sputnik" went into orbit the pressure in school has accelerated.

The First Methodist Church of Springfield, Illinois, is a downtown church that has drastically revised its program and approach to young people in timing and in depth. Its leadership has achieved one of the most dynamic youth programs I have seen. Each Wednesday night is reserved as youth night at the church. The young people come directly from school, expecting to spend at least four hours in study, fellowship, choir rehearsal, and worship. Here's how Wednesday evening is regularly scheduled:

3:30 p.m. *Study or fellowship:* The church provides two rooms, a fellowship room and a study room. If they want to talk, they go to the fellowship room. If they want to work on their homework, they may go to the study room.

4:30 p.m. *Choir rehearsal:* The youth choir is seen as a major service that young people render to the life of the church. An hour-and-a-half rehearsal is required each week.

6:00 p.m. *Snack:* Each person orders hamburgers which are brought in from a nearby hamburger stand. Drinks are available from the coke machine. There is no fuss.

6:30 p.m. *Worship:* These programs are kept flexible enough to meet the questions that young people are asking when they are asking them. The effort is to stimulate young people to ask the questions that need answering.

8:00 p.m. *Fellowship circle:* Often this closing prayer time takes the form of a "Love Feast." This is such an exciting breakthrough in helping young people to express acceptance and love for each other, that I want to describe the experience.

The group gathers in a circle with interlocking arms and hands. As they stand quietly in prayer, someone offers a prayer for God's blessing: "Dear heavenly Father, we give this circle to thee. . . ." Then the leader suggests that each person will pray for a meeting of their minds to see if there is someone in the group on whom they should focus their love and prayer. Soon someone is nominated as the one to be honored with loving appreciation. Later, it comes natural to remember others who are not present with intercessory prayer by name. The night I was their guest speaker in preparation for a Christian Witness Mission, Sue, the chairman of this effort, was nominated. Sue took her place in the chair of honor in the center. Joe stepped up behind her, laid his hands on her shoulders and said: "Sue, this is your brother in Christ, Joe. The Christ in me greets the Christ in you. I have only been in this group a short time. It doesn't take a person long to know you for it shows all the time."

Next a girl took her place behind Sue and said: "Sue, ever since I was in the eighth and ninth grades I have wanted to know you, and I made it a point to know you, and I'm glad I did for you have been a real sweet girl. I want to thank you for all the help you have been to me. Without you this group would not be what it is. Thank you for being what you are."

Another: "Ever since I have known you, I've looked up to you as someone I have admired. You have been a person who has helped me a whole lot."

A boy: "Sue, this is Dave. This is the third time I have come here. Yet you called me by name from the first. I thought that I could feel the presence of Christ in you."

The adult counselor: "The Christ in me says 'Hello!' to the Christ in you. I pray that God will continually use you for good. God love you and bless you through me."

By this time the presence of the Holy Spirit is a fact that each person feels. Pentecost becomes, not something that happened long ago in an upper room in Jerusalem, but young hearts strangely warmed in Old First's basement parlor every Wednesday night!

Here is a group that has created a new structure for a benediction in which love is not just a nice feeling, but a giving and receiving of love and appreciation one to another. Is it any wonder that the group hangs together with a cohesiveness and sense of belonging to one another that affirms the New Testament idea of being "members of one another"?

The Sunday night program at Springfield First takes the form of a spiritual renewal group. These renewal action groups like those of The Twelve, Yokefellow Movement, "Witnessing in Daily Life" groups, Koinonia groups, Icthus Fellowships, and other small face-to-face groups search for a first-hand encounter with Christ and one another. They seek for strength for faithful witness to and in the world. Their central purpose is not a cozy feeling of comfort but one of seeking to be God's people in the world. For Old First, the disciplined group provides the leadership that is providing both the knowledge and power of the gospel.

That which we have seen and heard we proclaim also to you, so that you may have fellowship with us.

—I John 1:3

3

TOWARD A VITAL YOUTH FELLOWSHIP

The teen-ager is the best instrument through which God can get through to other teen-agers. Always we have this problem—the uncommitted youth. We also have the answer: the person of Jesus Christ; but we do not always link problem and answer. The missing link is the committed teen-ager who is willing to witness to others, in all he says and does.

—Dick Gilbert[1]

The greatest stumbling block for the young person who makes his commitment to Christ is that he joins the church expecting to *do* something. Instead, he finds the church is stabbing at windmills. He feels out of place. He is confronted with no radical or relevant opportunity for service. He finds that "S.O.S" means the "Same Old Stuff."

Now, however, some radical changes are taking place. And the youth evangelism effort is in the forefront of this movement to bridge the gap between the contemporary church and the world. Young people find this movement in unconventional evangelism vital and exciting.

The renewal of the church is the work of the Holy Spirit, not of men. The call to those who have answered Christ's call is to a deeper commitment, a truer obedience. A new evangelism is emerging. The United Church Board of Homeland Ministries evangelism secretary, Gerald J. Jud, puts it this way: "In its broadest sense evangelism means all the gospel's traffic between the kingdom and the world; in its narrowest, all the church's efforts to tell and help the world hear the good news of God in Christ."

If the church is identified as the kingdom of God, then evangelism is getting people to enter this ark of salvation, to repent and be baptized and join the church: evangelism is getting the world into the church.

"If the church is seen as fundamentally a Christian presence in the world of man's work and play, evangelism is getting the church into the world." [2]

If we are to develop a vital youth fellowship, we must have a clear understanding of the scope and the great themes of the Christian faith. It is impossible to separate Christian faith and works, theory and practice. We can't separate the power of the gospel from the facts of the gospel. Evangelism is God's creative action in everything we know or do. We must be willing to do our homework on these themes. Never before have the themes of the Christian faith been stated as clearly or concisely as in the comprehensive curriculum plan now used as the design for Christian studies in Protestant churches. The facts of the gospel as we know them are all here. We must be willing to learn what the Christian faith believes about man (life and its setting); God (the meaning and experience of revelation); Christ (redemption); vocation (discipleship); the church (Christian community). These are the great themes of the new curriculum for youth. An adequate youth evangelism must deal with the full spectrum of needs and goals of young people. [3]

We must have a careful understanding not only of the gospel but also of the persons to whom the gospel is addressed. For some time,

Christian workers with youth have felt the need of a statement of objectives for use in the Christian education of young people. Here such a statement is offered in the hope that it will stimulate study, discussion, and sharing of ideas and reactions. As you read it, ask: How does this statement relate the gospel to the world the senior high lives in?

As persons are aware of God's self-disclosure and seeking love in Jesus Christ and respond in faith and love, they come to know who they really are—sons of God (as redeemed sinners who in Christ may fulfill the meaning of personality)—and what their human situation (past, present, and future) means; grow as sons of God rooted in the Christian community (the Church); live in the Spirit of God in every relationship (the heart of the matter in ethics and social responsibility); fulfill their common discipleship—implying stewardship—in the world (the family, the community, and the larger society); and abide in the Christian hope.[4]

These are the first steps for young Christians in search of a vital youth fellowship in Christ.[5] While our mission is in the world, our mission station is the church. If our training for evangelism doesn't go on continuously, the work of evangelism will not get done at all.

If we are to share the gospel with others, we must know what that gospel is. Ask your youth group to face the question: "What do we have to share with those outside the church that will make a difference in our lives?"

Young people who are searching for adequate answers to these questions about these life-long concerns are demonstrating that such creative activity can build bridges of understanding and fellowship between youth inside and those outside the church. When such dialogue begins, communication opens up, Christian action makes the gospel come alive, and commitment becomes a possibility.

Following are some bridge-building ventures toward a more vital church undertaken by young Christians and their adult counselors in the hope that persons who might never set foot inside a church building will see religion in action and will ask the questions: Why are you doing this? What's the church up to, anyway? And then the Christian can give his Christian testimony to his faith.

Unconventional Experiments Toward a Vital Youth Ministry[6]

Everywhere you see evidence of the work of an increasing number of venturesome youth and adult workers who are in training and preparation for the twenty-first century. Their purpose is to change local churches everywhere with what Hans Margull calls "a move from come-structures to go-structures." Here are a few of the most venturesome and significant. As you read these brief reports, ask yourself: Where is our mission field? What are the things that need doing that we could do in our own Lambaréné or intentional community?

Here are some creative and challenging ways churches are attempting to bridge the gap between the church and the contemporary world to make the Christian faith vital and relevant to young people.

These efforts in Christian missionary service move in three directions: first, in outreach to youth themselves in their teen culture; secondly, in service to the community at large; and thirdly, in service and training beyond the local church and community.

Penetrating the High School Community with the Gospel

Sparked by the Youth Exploration of The Methodist Church, churches in Muncie and Kokomo, Indiana, cooperated in an exploratory project to penetrate the high school community. The effort enlisted the youth of the churches with the help and guidance of the full-time director, a Vanderbilt School of Theology student who took a year out of his studies for the Muncie venture. The experiment focused on the high school community through the Christian youth. The purpose was to "help the youth of the church discern their discipleship in the school and to live with the greatest degree of meaning in their own school community."

The project included buzz groups during lunch hours and after school, united fellowship activities, training of youth counselors, discussion groups on movies and literature, vocations conferences, rallies, prayer groups, family church school classes, hootenannies, and minister's meetings. A number of adults kept personal diaries to define for themselves personal answers to the question: What does it mean to be a salty Christian in the world? The greatest accomplishment: helping Christian youth and teachers to know one another and work together as Christians across local church and high school lines.

The Coffee House Movement

Philadelphia's Seventh Heaven Coffee House is one of the many mission outposts comprising a dramatic and widespread movement in unconventional evangelism. The coffee house offers a place to meet and talk in a climate of openness of thought and feeling. Young people are selected and trained to serve as waiters and hosts. Low-key program features include: artists, performers, films, dramatic skits, and forums. The climate is one of give and take. The coffee house movement serves as an extension of the mission of the church in the role of servant.

In New York City, the coffee house served as a forum after the race riots to formulate suggestions for a crash program to provide training, jobs and recreation for Negro youth.[7]

Teen-Age Nightclub

Central Methodist Mission's Cabaret in Sydney, Australia, is the world's most famous Christian Saturday night nightclub. But the idea is getting around. Los Angeles, Seattle, and dozens of other centers are experimenting. The New York State Youth Commission offers suggestions. The Sydney version of church-sponsored nightclubs features a combo, popular vocalists, traditional hymns with a jazz setting, and a brief and challenging call to commitment to Christ.[8]

Youth Emphasis Week

The annual Youth Emphasis Week in Malden, Missouri, is an attempt at saturation of the community, with the high school as the focal point. A student-council faculty committee plans the week with representatives of all the religious groups of the community. The students raise ques-

31

tions in advance for the visiting guest to speak to and discuss in an open forum. They include: "Personal Integrity," "Human Relations," and "Patriotism—Americanism, Communism."

High School Summer Assistants

To encourage potential candidates for the ministry, The First Methodist Church of Sturgeon Bay, Wisconsin, employs high school students as summer assistants, working closely with the pastor.

Committee to Avert Dropouts

In Fort Worth, a vigilant committee of white and Negro youth from all the churches have organized to check each week on the dropouts from the high schools and to talk to them and try to persuade them to reenter school and finish their education. Dropouts will often listen to other young people where adult counselors can't get through.

Work with Juvenile Delinquents and Social Deviants

The youth who are in trouble with the law and the society in which they live are the responsibility of the church. The extent to which young people can enter into the complex social problems of the vicious poverty cycle may be limited. Christian young people can offer the young person in trouble something that no judge or parent or social worker or minister can offer: acceptance and understanding of his peer group. And this is often where the youngster in trouble is stiff-armed and hurt the most.

What can we do for persons in trouble? We can care. As others accept him he accepts himself. And we can come to understand the problem and get involved when we are needed.[9]

Recreational Leadership for Blighted Neighborhoods

Tampa Heights, Florida, young people have developed a recreational program in a blighted neighborhood of Negro and white families. They have helped build an outdoor basketball court and playground and are at work raising funds for gym mats for tumbling.

Aid to Crippled Children

Volunteer youth and adults may serve as counselors, teachers, and companions to handicapped children. Volunteers may teach arts and crafts, help plan parties, help with music, dramatics, and nature study. Any Crippled Children's Society has need for more volunteers than they can find.

The Church in Mission Along Pasadena Parade Route

A committee of Pasadena churchmen and representatives of youth- and community-serving agencies, including the YMCA, the police department, a theological seminary, a radio station, and the council of churches united to provide "Let's Talk" coffee houses. Volunteers operated them all night on the eve of the annual New Year's Day Rose Parade in Pasadena. High school youth in great numbers spent all night in "slumber parties" along Colorado Street, saving front row seats for the big event. Fifteen all night church-sponsored coffee houses offered coffee, folk songs, skilled youth workers, and a chance to talk about any subject. The minister of education who sparked the venture says: "It seems to me this is the kind of a venture the church must increasingly engage in. For too long we have simply waited for people to come to us. We must take the initiative and go where the people are —to listen to what they have to say to us."

Evangelism on the Beach

Christian youth in the San Diego District became concerned about the vast numbers of teen-agers on the Pacific beaches during Holy Week, which is spring vacation for the high schools. Since only a small percentage of Californians are church members, they assumed the beach was ripe for mission. The youth who planned the endeavor spurned using famous faces and well-known voices as bait. One girl protested: "Isn't it better for nobodies to tell other nobodies what Christ means to them?"

Strategy included hootenannies, song-fests, campfires, games, and food on the beach, an open invitation to join the crowd. Quiet times in the nearby church building, where the unconventional evangelists lived in sleeping bags at night and studied their basics during the mornings, kept them on their toes for the no-holds-barred encounter on the beach every afternoon and evening.

Candy-stripers

Hospitals are glad to have high school girls, many of whom aspire to be registered nurses, for volunteer service in hospitals. They are known as "Candy-stripers" because of their distinctive uniforms. Your hospital can give you information.

Teen-Agers in the Civil Rights Issue

From the beginning of the Civil Rights movement, teen-agers, junior highs and high school students, as well as college students, have taken the lead in the sit-ins and demonstrations on the street. In Nashville, Tennessee, for instance, where a community has changed its mind about the race issue in an incredibly short time, young people were the first to "hit the bricks" in demonstrations demanding integration of the downtown theaters and eating facilities. Young people are willing and able to take risks where their elders hesitate to move.

Intentional Communities

These voluntary projects sponsored by the National Conference of the Methodist Youth Fellowship, enlist students sixteen to twenty years of age. For ten weeks persons from unbelievably diverse backgrounds come together as strangers to work in day camps, low-income housing projects, the head-start program, playgrounds and preschool playrooms. Two persons designated as "stewards" may work as common laborers to help support the community while others work as volunteers. Openness and honesty are the prerequisites as the "family" stands before one another in despair, anger, hostility, fear, mistrust, confession, repentance, and rebirth.

Christian Witness Workcamps

Fifty high school students from Arizona and California give new meaning to the traditional evangelism concept each summer through service in two annual summer nine-day Christian Witness Workcamps. The projects move each year as new needs arise. The young people pay for the privilege of attending the workcamps. They are bedded down on air mattresses in Sunday school rooms at night, eat, together in the church hall, meet together for training and inspiration in three class sessions and prayer groups each day.

The rest of the time they spend knocking on doors and pounding pavements. The teams divide to serve in communities where they help call on people who are not active in church. Volunteers work in areas of need as evangelists who answer the call, "Come over and help us."

Summer Evangelists

The General Board of Evangelism of The Methodist Church offers training and secures employment for theological students for two months of summer service. Trainees are given two weeks of intensive orientation and practice in evangelism. Many of the young evangelists serve in their own local communities. Others serve across the nation as day camp workers and counselors in the inner city as ministers to youth and as chaplains in recreational areas. In a recent summer they came from twelve seminaries, forty states and nine countries.

Invest Your Summer

Your church has a job for you this summer. For information, order this year's ecumenical catalogue of service opportunities *Invest Your Summer* published by the Commission on Youth Service Projects. If you are willing to accept the disciplines and share fully the life of the group, you may be able to work with migrant children; work for a year in Africa or Asia; exchange homes and schools with a student in Europe for a year in the International Youth Exchange; or work with crippled children.[10]

Weekend Work Camps

Weekends provide an opportunity to create bridges of understanding between suburban youth and inner-city youth in Philadelphia. These service projects developed out of the coffee house project where suburban and inner-city youth meet on Friday evenings. On Saturday youth from the parish come together for orientation and a field trip on foot or in a bus. Then youth are involved in directing activities that lead them into observation and research with neighborhood children. Their assignment is to discover how they can work with children and what their mothers want for their children: What kind of playground activities? Would mothers help supervise? Should play be open to all or limited to members? Young people have learned to be full partners in the ministry of this inner-city parish.[11]

The Break with Traditional Evangelism

You can see from this brief overview of youth evangelism and these unconventional experiments toward a more vital youth ministry that something new is taking place in the field of evangelism. A fresh crop of young church leaders has arisen who are dissatisfied with the traditional forms and programs of evangelism. These innovators are determined to retool the evangelistic strategy of the churches, making it more relevant to this generation.[12] These young men believe that the church has a redemptive message to give the world, but since the world does not seem to be listening, they feel the message needs a new wave length. Youth seem to be tuned in, for they have learned to listen on the run with a portable earphone.

Novel experiments, however, are not enough. Renewal in the church can come when we who are the church learn genuinely to love each other as Christ loves us. Then we may see our mission is to love the world as God loves it.

Freely ye have received, freely give.

—MATT. 10:8 (KJV)

4

WHY SHOULD I WITNESS?

Evangelism is relating to my neighbor in such a way that I come to care for him, understand him, and speak to him that he may know, trust, love, and obey God in Christ.

—HOWARD W. ELLIS AND TED McEACHERN [1]

Our motives for evangelism can never be the same since Reuel Howe's rediscovery of *The Miracle of Dialogue*. The transforming power of dialogue-in-relationship has given a new and deeper meaning to Christian witness. Christian witness is love in action. Dr. Howe says:

Dialogue is to love, what blood is to the body. When the flow of blood stops, the body dies. When dialogue stops, love dies and resentment and hate are born. But dialogue can restore a dead relationship. Indeed, this is the miracle of dialogue: it can bring relationship into being, and it can bring into being once again a relationship that has died. [2]

The Motivation of Friendship

All of us know the gnawing emptiness of loneliness. And we also know the warmth of human friendship. More than anything else, conversion is like a growing and maturing friendship. Deep friendships do not just happen. They are made. One step leads to another. Think of the friendship that means most to you. How did it happen?

1. *I reach out to him.* A friendship begins when we open the door of our lives and welcome another person in. We may learn about him long before we meet him face-to-face, through something we have heard, or something he has written or said. Some of the people who influence us most may be persons we have not yet known through a formal introduction. A formal introduction may not be the best way to really know a person anyhow. It may keep us apart. Meeting a person and really knowing him is the difference between rubbing shoulders with a person in a lonely crowd and being aware of him in personal conversation. With the preliminary step of personal introduction we usually make up our minds whether we will make the further effort to know this person and let him know us.

2. *He responds to me.* Do we really want to take the risk of knowing one another? Are we willing to get involved? Maybe we aren't sure. So we put on a mask at first, perhaps a great big friendly mask. But we are careful to try to make an impression. We guard our words. We are careful what we say. We keep thinking of what he may think of us. Can we trust him? Does he trust us? Maybe if he comes to know us as we really are he won't like us. So we engage in small talk. We are careful not to get into depth dialogue.

The breakthrough comes when one or both of us decides to go farther. Something about the other makes us want to know who he is, what he feels, how he sees life. And something tells us he wants to know us. So we plunge into a kind of a game of exploration. "This is me. Who are you?" We may really want to know. Or maybe we don't. But we are willing to test our potential friendship.

3. *We learn to know each other.* When we are willing to let the

other person know us, we may come to know him. If we want love we must love. If we want the other's attention, we must give him our attention. Persons who would know and be known as mutual friends must be God's instruments of love in human relation. They must speak —and listen. We let the other person see where we stand, what we think, and how we feel. And we are open to discover where he stands, what he thinks, and how he feels—if he wants me to know him. The way I respond to him has a lot to do with the way he responds to me. I not only have a friend. I become one.

The Theology of Christian Fellowship

There is a theological motivation that is at work, too, in the work of evangelism. The true motivation for Christian witness is the incarnation of his Spirit in the lives of man. If we are to know Christ and one another we must take the facts of the gospel seriously. Through his presence and the working of his Spirit, God is carrying on a divine friendship with man. And man may respond to that friendship.

1. *In the Incarnation, God reaches out to us.* God seems to have the same problem we have: the problem of communication. If we could read God's diary, we might find an entry that read something like this: "How can I, the eternal God, get through to mortal man with all of his limitations of time and space and an animal-like body?" God seems to have solved his problem in the Incarnation. In Christ we have a picture of what God means for man to be. Here is the perfect portrait. We see it, we love to look at it, to hear about it, to read about it. The Incarnation is God meeting us face to face in a personal introduction of the life of God in the life of man. We are to incarnate his Spirit for our time, as Jesus was God incarnate when he walked in the flesh among us.

2. *In the Crucifixion, Christ accepts us in spite of our hostility.* The cross brings us into fellowship. The Crucifixion stabs us with the painful realization that Christ who was born a baby died as a man accused of blasphemy and high treason. By accepting the unacceptable, loving the unloving, he accepted the cross. "Were you there when they

crucified my Lord?" the Negro spiritual asks. And I reply: "My God! I was not only there. I did it! This is the kind of persons we are!" The Crucifixion is God's great self-revelation. God let his son die rather than violate the freedom that he has entrusted to us as sons of God. Like a father, he accepts us, in spite of our unacceptability. The fellowship of Christians, then, accepts death and life, cruelty and pain, joy and disappointments, knowing that nothing, not even death, can separate us from the love of God. At the cross we are reminded that the new creation requires suffering. We have a God who knows all about us and cares for us anyway! That is grace.

3. *In the Resurrection, we become one with him.* In the risen Christ, God brushes aside death itself and presents his Son in person as God himself sees and knows him. The resurrection is the world's greatest unsolved mystery story. But the clue to solving the story is the simple fact that the living Christ appears only to his firends. Only the inner group of disciples and friends who had lived with him, loved him, seen him die, ever saw him again. It is only as I become his friend that I can know the living Christ or receive his Spirit. Here in this divine friendship, then, I discover who I am, and what I am meant to be. For God is trying to perform the same miracle in me that he accomplished in Jesus Christ!

The Deeper Motivation

A vital youth program must deal with the full spectrum of the needs and goals of young people. In this struggle for identity which the Christian believes is found in Christ, three deep hungers of the human heart emerge. They are: the hunger "to be," "to belong," and "to do." If the good news we affirm meets these heart hungers at the deepest level, we can speak with some confidence of redemption or salvation of the whole person. What does the Christian fellowship have to offer youth in their hunger for "being," "belonging," and "doing"?

1. *I become what I am because of my commitment.* To this desire "to be" someone, to be recognized as a person of value, to discover selfhood, the Christian faith says: "In this search for identity, you are

40

not alone. You have a model. This model is Jesus Christ. He is a preview of coming attractions. God is trying to perform the same miracle of Christian perfection in your life that he performed in Jesus Christ."

Young people are searching for identity. "Who am I?" is the persistent question they are asking in a thousand ways. The truth of who we are potentially is revealed in Jesus Christ. We do not become Christians by accident. Destiny is not a matter of chance. It is a matter of choice. Evangelism offers a choice—a commitment to a person.

The cover for a sassy, unconventional evangelistic leaflet shows a strong man flexing his muscles and asks the question: Who's your hero? A young person flipping the cover to the inside pages is confronted with Christ. We discover who we are when we discover who he is. And to find him we must want him with all our hearts. That's commitment.

2. *I discover that I belong because I am in community.* Every person desires "to belong" to those who will accept him. The first thing the Christian faith says to a person is: "You are not alone. You belong. You are a part of an endless line of splendor, of men and women who down through the centuries have given their lives to the church." In our fragmented world, a sense of the nature and mission of the church as a caring community does not just happen. Such care and concern must be structured. In the youth ministry of the church where young people may know and be known, masks can come off as young people get to know others as they are—and come to care for one another anyway. This is grace in action.

The word "fellowship" is distinctively a Christian term. It is not in the vocabulary of the outsider. It has an honored history: "fellows-in-the-ship"—an "all-in-the-same-boat-feeling." Here is Christ's call to "come after me and I will make you fishers of men." In a world where so many forces pull us apart and alienate us from others, the church today stands high, something like an aircraft carrier to which ships may return after they have launched out in mission.

3. *I discover that life counts when I accept my commission.* Every person desires "to do" something that will count—something

41

that will give purpose to his life. Young people are asking some critical questions and dreaming great dreams. They want to know: What is the meaning of human life? How can I get the most out of life? When we think of Christ's answer to these questions, we think of the Great Commission: "All authority in heaven and on earth has been given to me. Go therefore and make disciples." (Matt. 28:18-20.)

We do not know what the future holds. We live in faith that God's purpose is revealed in the authority of the living Christ. His is a call to prepare for and share in the kingdom of God. We are responding to that call most surely when we go out in the world to bear witness to Jesus Christ. And the world for the teen-ager is the world of the high school, the football field, the classroom, the hangout, the home.

The Personal Motivation

We are never really able to witness until we have another person in our minds and on our hearts. Sharing the Christ we know with others is the most intensely personal dialogue we can know. Like marriage, "it is not to be entered into unadvisedly, but reverently, discreetly, and in the fear of God." Marriage is simply a heightened and continuous friendship. The dynamics of friendship provide us with our guidelines for evangelism, "love in action." Friendship always begins with an introduction.

So, let me ask you to begin your venture in witnessing by thinking of a person whom, so far as you know, is outside the life and influence of the church. Or maybe he is a dropout. Perhaps he has never discovered the church at all. He does not think of the church as a friendly or open fellowship. He's out. You know this. And you know him well enough to talk to him. Introductions are over. Now, think of him as a potential Christian. You are the missionary. He is your missionary assignment. Hold it! Have you got your assignment? His name? His address? Write it down in the margin of this book before you go any farther. Got it? Okay. You can't enter into dialogue without someone else on the other end of the line.

All right. You have a face before you—a stranger to Christ. And you'd like to introduce him to Christ, or maybe serve as a reconciler. Perhaps if you do not become his friend and speak the necessary word, he will always be a stranger to the sense of purpose that comes from "being," "belonging," and "doing" that you have come to feel in the Christian fellowship.

Now before you speak to him, ask yourself these questions: What kind of a Christian am I? What kind of image does he have of me? What do I know about him? How does he feel about our youth fellowship?

Does he feel: This is my group, or this is their group? Does he feel: *My* church; *my* pastor; *my* Christ? Does he think about our relationship in the first person, or in the third person? Evangelism is the process of moving from the third person to the first person in all the relationships that matter. Love in action—that's our motive for witnessing.

And our fellowship is with the Father and with his Son Jesus Christ.

—I John 1:3

5

GET THEM ON YOUR HEARTS

Whatever you do, respect personality. It is wrong to treat persons as puppets to be pushed or pulled or propositioned. They must be persuaded by the power of the spirit. —Fred Cloud

We've seen that evangelism begins with a concern for persons. We must see that the ultimate purpose of the youth program is to lead youth to commitment to Christ. If we are to witness clearly, we must clarify our motives. We must be committed to Christ ourselves if we are to lead others in his way. And our youth program must be a vital program—one that bridges the gap between friendship and evangelism. Now we are ready to seek out the outsiders.

Finding prospects is largely a matter of imagination. Take a young pastor we'll call Ray Christian. Ray came as the student minister of a country church in Iowa.

"Where are the young people?" Ray asked.

His church-school superintendent—call him Phillip—said, "We don't have any young people."

The pastor persistently took pencil and paper. "Give me the names of our church families."

44

"Well, there's the Johnsons—Alvin."

"Any children?"

"Yes, there's Susanna, she's nine, and Louise, she's fifteen, and Bob, he's about twelve or thirteen."

"Louise and Bob—Who's next?"

"Well, there's the Poindexters. They have Paul—"

Phillip named twenty young people. Ray Christian listed them.

"Look!" Ray said. "We have enough young people to build up a fine youth fellowship!"

"But," Phillip said, "we don't have any young people!"

There they were—twenty young people as Phillip had named them—but he still didn't see them!

How do you find them?

Before you begin listing names, get this point:

No person is a prospect until his name goes through the hands and heart and mind of another young person!

1. *Begin with your own young people.* Enlist the cooperation of the entire church. You have many sources of information. But a name is not a prospect until some person begins plotting and praying that he may be guided into the Christian way. Prepare your lists carefully. Later you'll assign each name to the person most interested in reaching him. Get them on your hearts; then put them on your list.

2. *Check your church constituency for teen-agers who are not professing Christians.* This may be your best source of prospects. Get people alerted for names of young people. Your church membership secretary can help you. Who attends? Who does not attend?

A West Coast pastor started a church in a schoolhouse. He now has 600 members. He said, "I don't depend on surveys for prospects."

"But," I said, "how do you get prospects?" His church is crowded with people. His people have built a new church, dedicated a modern parsonage. His youth group is growing and overflowing with enthusiasm. He is a real evangelist-pastor-educator.

He says, "We start with the families closest to us. Then we work out from there. If we move out and bring in those who are closest to us, others will move in from the perimeter. As they move in, others come seeking the source of this new-found power."

3. *Make a survey of your schools.* Student organizations, the Hi-Y or the student council, sometimes take on a survey of religious preference as a service project. Sometimes the character guidance program of your schools will open doors. School people vary widely in the cooperation they feel they can give to a survey. Don't exert pressure.

As a last resort, try Denver's system. The prospect chairman says, "We got our names from the school annuals. We finally listed 1,300 prospects. We got all the information we could from someone who knew each person. It was a tremendous job. We ran a Bureau of Missing Persons for weeks!"

I like that! Each church should have its Bureau of Missing Persons!

A rural pastor says, "We locate our lost sheep by taking an inventory of the school buses. One of our students was assigned to each bus."

The point is: *You can get them if you want them.*

4. *Take a quick house-to-house survey of teen-agers only.* The young people ask, "Do you have any teen-agers here? Where do they attend church?"

In Topeka a suburban church set a record for recruiting youth by this method. They found 315 prospects in one week. They enlisted 120 new young people for the church and their youth fellowship. The adult counselor said, "What will we do? We need four new youth fellowship groups!"

5. *Conduct a religious survey of your community.* A complete community survey takes careful planning. Begin weeks in advance. If possible put responsibility in the hands of your ministerial association. Offer to help. People respond better to a religious census when they learn that all the churches are working together on it.

You can secure information on planning a religious census by writing your interdenominational headquarters.[1] Your local council of churches can help you. Of course, you can always print your own census cards. But the prepared packets will give all the materials you will need. And they save time and trouble.

A raw, unprocessed list is a beginning, but your list must have tender loving care before it becomes a responsibility list. You may not have a prospect list at all; you may have a *prospective* prospect list.

Let me repeat: *No person is a prospect until he is on the heart and mind of some other person. Get them on your hearts; then put them on your list.*

How Do You Get to Know Them?

The cultivation of persons as friends is as important in evangelism as courtship is in marriage. You can't emphasize this enough. Without this warming-up process of preevangelism, prospects aren't really prospects; they are only *prospective* prospects.

Young people can be won without their realizing they have been the objects of evangelism—like the fellow who falls in love gradually. He may not realize he's been pursued. That's the way it ought to be. Subtle.

Most people fall in step with the Christian way gradually. It is hard for them to point to the time when they first realized there was One walking with them on the way. Or maybe their conversion experience was sudden—in a single moment. And they can say: "For me that was it. My life has never been the same." For some, Christian conversion is a head-over-heels experience—like love at first sight. And like true love, the experience must grow.

Christian principles are at stake in the art of sex, love, and marriage. That's true of the art of winning people to the church, too. Somebody— I'm glad I can't remember who—said, "There's no bad way to make a Christian!" How naïve can we get? The only way to make Christians is in a Christian way.

Farrell D. Jenkins puts it this way:

Evangelism is not a business; it is a romance. We need to carry into our church program the same evangelistic warmth that we used when we proposed to our sweetheart. We did not coldly analyze her personality and state that she needed our personality to complement hers. Just so, evangelism is not content to coldly psychoanalyze people. It is a proposal to them that the Lord Christ loves them with . . . undying care, and that He yearns for their love in return. There must be *warmth, intelligence,* and *love* in our evangelism.[2]

Maybe we're hesitant to list the steps of procedure, because winning people to Christ is such a sacred undertaking. Remember the only reason we have literature on love, courtship, and marriage—and on personal evangelism—is so that God may have a chance to change the lives of people.

So let's put down some effective steps in what we might call pre-evangelism. How do we get them on our hearts?

1. *Make sure you really want them.* Ask yourself: What is our attitude toward these outsiders? Would they feel welcome if they came? Would we be glad and willing to have them as a part of our group?

You can be sure your group has the big idea when somebody says, "You know, I think I ought to talk to Dick. He's got some real problems. I have an idea I might help him."

Get them on your hearts; then put them on your list.

2. *Think of your group as a redemptive fellowship.* This is the way Wally Chappell describes a Christian fellowship:

In a Christian fellowship persons care about each other. Each person is concerned that every other person feels welcome and is a part of the group. In a Christian fellowship, young people understand one another; have patience with one another; accept one another.

Because there are so many factors that prevent fellowship, it will not come by accident. Many people must work and pray for Christian fellowship.

Your youth fellowship should be a laboratory in human relations. Your planning sessions and committee work offer opportunities for Christian fellowship.[3]

You see how it works out? Christian fellowship is a spirit, an atmosphere of fellow feeling. You find it in your work projects, your prayer groups, your planning committees, your study, your mealtime fun, your worship and recreation.

Get this big idea into the thinking of your officers, then into your group. Talk it over. Take an honest look at yourselves. Do your visitors want to come back? Do you care if they do? Do all your regulars feel that they belong? Do you want your fellowship to be one that gets hold of young persons and really redeems them from loneliness and lack of purpose in life? Do you want a redemptive fellowship?

3. *Specialize in friendliness.* Name tags help people get acquainted. When you have just a few newcomers, the name tags are really for *them* to learn the old timers. Print the first name big and readable.

More important for breaking the ice is the spirit of the regulars. Let them mix and mingle, visit and chat, with the newcomers. Go out of your way to make them feel at home. Forget your old buddies for the time being. Go after the new ones. Help the newcomer know two or three persons well and the names of many more.

One youth president says, "We have an unwritten law. No one ever goes home alone. Every person always leaves with a congenial group."

4. *Take Christian fellowship into your boy-girl relationships.* "Witnessing can be done in so many ways," Roy L. Smith says in an article, "Effective Witnessing." [4] He tells this true story:

He was a youth quite without any knowledge of the church, any acquaintanceship with religion, or any thought of God. His home had been broken up when he was but a small boy as a result of a combination of liquor and infidelity.

She was a vivacious girl, conscientious in her faith, and devoted to her church. . . . She was trying to be a Christian.

By one of those strange circumstances for which there seems to be no explanation, the irreligious lad became acquainted with the religious girl and was greatly attracted to her. On the occasion of his first opportunity he asked her for a date.

"I'll be glad to go with you on Saturday night," the girl replied, with an ingratiating smile, "provided you will go to church with me on Sunday morning."

This was the beginning of their romance and his Christian experience. Today they are married. He stands in the pulpit of a midwestern church.

"It all started," he says, "because she said, 'I'll go with you on Saturday night if you will go to church with me on Sunday morning.' "

How Do You Go After Them?

1. *Infiltrate your normal social groups.* Some of your most effective witnessing is done informally. Some youth groups call their infiltration movement "The 3-C's"—for "Christ-centered Conversation." They don't repeat pious platitudes. They don't preach in the corridors at school. But they do try to bring Christ into their conversation naturally. Christians around the world call this technique "gossiping the gospel."

Take a small town in Southern Indiana which we'll call Richland. The Richland church has a booming youth group. These youth have the one organized young people's group in town. Everybody goes. How do they get the good news to others?

Let the Christian witness chairman, a girl we'll call Sharon Church, tell you: "We use the locker room and the classrooms for 'gossiping the gospel.' What I mean is, we manage to talk about the youth program and activities. A little group of us gets together in the hall. We start talking about what we're doing and planning. Soon a crowd gathers. We keep them interested in what we're doing by making our church work a lively topic of conversation."

"Our buzz groups are natural centers of information. Even the boys are getting to be good talkers," Sharon Church says. "Our boys say, 'Boys don't gossip. Boys just exchange information.' "

2. *Get witnessing on a person-to-person basis.* Two-by-two evangelism is fine. But it isn't personal enough and consistent enough to reach some people. Encourage your young people to witness informally. Turn them loose.

In Los Angeles teen-agers have gasoline in their blood. People call them "hot-rodders." But when they get religion, they're hard to beat. Let me tell you about the Los Angeles boy we'll call Abe Atkins.

Abe was one of the hundreds of young people who came to our interdenominational youth rally in the Shrine Auditorium one night a few years ago. A youth choir sang. A pastel painting of Sallman's "Head of Christ" was the worship center of the evening.

Many young people streamed forward in response to the challenge to commitment at the close of the service. We handed out to each young person a pocket-size copy of Sallman's portrait of Christ.

Abe stuck his picture on the windshield of his "crate."

A few days after Abe put on his new accessory, one of his friends, a boy we'll call Jim, got in with him. Jim saw that Abe had added something new.

"Say," said Jim, "who's the whiskered gent?"

"That's Jesus Christ," Abe said.

"Oh," said Jim. He'd heard the name.

Abe told his friend about Christ. He told him simply what the Christian faith meant to him. Abe sold Jim on the idea of living for Christ. He convinced him. Jim changed his ways. He joined Abe's church.

And then this happened—this sequel: The Sunday Jim joined the church was a never-to-be-forgotten commencement day for him. Yet Jim's parents didn't feel that way. They weren't in church when Jim was baptized and joined the church.

Jim came home to dinner. His father reached for the bread. Jim reached for his arm.

"We haven't said grace," Jim said. "May we?"

Then before his family had time to recover from the shock, Jim bowed his head. He said a prayer he'd learned that morning from *The Upper Room.*

"Now pass the bread," he said.

This is what happens when you get the church out of its four walls into the highways and hedges. If you want to develop disciples: *Get witnessing on a person-to-person basis.*

3. *Write a personal letter of invitation to each prospect.* Letters

are important to young people. Make your letter personal, informal, chatty—like this:

CENTRAL COMMUNITY CHURCH
Blankville, Illinois

Hi, there!

We hope you're going to be home this weekend. For you see, there are two big events you'll want to be counted in on. To come right out with it, we want to have the opportunity to visit you; and we want you to visit us.

We're making friendly calls this weekend on every young person we know who is interested in joining our youth fellowship. Maybe you've wondered, "How does a person join the youth fellowship?"

We'd like to tell you about our fellowship. Maybe you'd be interested in our drama group, our fellowship times, our prayer cell groups, our regular worship and study times Sunday morning and evening. We'd like to tell you about them.

And maybe you've wondered, "What does a Christian believe? What does a Christian do? What does a Christian stand for?" This enclosed folder, *Becoming Christian*[5] will help answer your questions. We hope you'll read it carefully.

Some of our members will be calling on you this week end. We want to be sure to see you. We'll try to visit you Friday night or sometime Saturday. If you're busy, let us know and we'll call back Sunday or sometime at your earliest convenience.

The second thing is this: We're planning a special event for you and your parents Sunday evening at the church from 7:00 P.M. to 9:00 P.M. This is your personal invitation. Please come—and bring your parents. This is their invitation, too!

Cordially yours,

Harriet Love
Youth President

4. *Stage a "come-as-you-are" day for all youth.* This is an effective way of rounding up your newcomers.

Here's the way it worked in Skokie, Illinois, the youth president reporting: "Details were secret. Only the youth council was in on the know. We kept our plans under wraps. We called this Sunday 'CAYA-DAY.' We advertised it in our bulletin, talked it up at school. At 4:00 P.M. Sunday the officers called on the regulars. Each officer with a car took off with five to ten names. At each home we said: 'Get your car and come-as-you-are!'

"Then the regulars picked up the kids on our constituency list and our new prospects. We brought in 185 of them. We personally escorted each one to church. One of our fellows showed up in a baker's uniform."

The western theme is popular. The slogan: "Rope 'em, tie 'em, and break 'em!" Tall Texas tales, chuck-wagon "chow," and blue jeans are the rule.

"Come-as-you-are" days break out of church into the highways and hedges!

5. *Provide a youth center.* Your church may do wonderful things with a teen canteen or youth center.[6] Take a small-town church in Ohio. Here's a young pastor just out of seminary who says, "We saw no reason why the youth room at the church should be closed six days a week. Our church kids needed a 'hangout.' We thought the church was the best meeting place for teens.

"We talked it over in the council. We got it before the group. We enlisted the backing of the adults and church officers. We went to the parents.

"We took time with youth and adults of the community to ask: Why do we want a teen canteen? Who is expected to come? What are the regulations? Rules of membership? Membership fee? How much scheduled time is informal? How much formal? What equipment do we need? How will the board of directors be related to the youth fellowship?"

Experienced youth leaders say, "Though you may regret to face it, ask, 'What will be done with those who ignore the rules?'"

Don't expect recreation and teen centers to do everything for you. Recreation is no substitute for other activities: worship, study, drama, discussion, program planning, evangelism, missions. And before you go overboard on recreation, this statement by Dick Gilbert, who is responsible for the national evangelistic program for Presbyterian youth, is worth considering:

It is poor strategy to have a social or mixer as the first introduction of newcomers to the Christian fellowship. It is far better to get acquainted and then invite them to a Sunday evening meeting especially pegged for them. In this way we come out fighting clean about our purpose with no dishonest implications about: "Come to Christ and it won't hurt a bit!"

Valuable as recreation is in the youth program of the church, recreation is not enough. The danger of a recreational program is that we often use recreation as "bait." Prospects may take our bait and leave us empty-handed. If they do, we will fish all night and take nothing!

This is worth repeating one more time: *Get them on your hearts; then put them on your list.*

As for you, always be steady, endure suffering, do the work of an evangelist, fulfill your ministry.

—II Tim. 4:5

6

HOW TO MAKE AN IMPACT

Master, Thou hast set before me an open door—the door to the human heart. Help me by winsomeness and love to enter the door of my friend's heart. Then help me to introduce him to my other Friend. If opportunities do not come easily, then help me to make them. If friends are not anxious and yearning, help me by my very call and life to create within them a craving and yearning. In his name. Amen.

—Andrew W. Kurth[1]

There's no doubt about it: Visitation evangelism does something in the lives of Christian young people which nothing else will do.

One pastor puts it this way: "You can cultivate all you want to with education. But if you're going to have a harvest, you must plant the seed. The seed is evangelism."

Will visitation evangelism work? That's like asking: Will a spade work?

Take a country parish. Here's a boy who hesitates to call on a neighbor boy he knows well. What happens? Let the boy tell you. He says, "Our friendship turned out to be an advantage!"

Now a downtown situation. People are scattered. They have no compact parish. Young people go to several schools. Older youth are in offices, classrooms, rooming houses. The pastor says, "We would have been lost long ago without visitation evangelism!"

A suburban church: "Visitation is the lifeblood of our church! We started with nothing. Every member we have came because someone sought him out and went to see him!"

Will young people talk about religion readily? The answer is "Yes." They talk about their faith because they're interested in knowing more about it. Young people will often tell each other things they haven't discussed with their parents.

Visitation evangelism on a youth-to-youth basis simply organizes this fellow feeling young people have for others. Everything you do by way of planning, organization, and training is for the purpose of helping one young person confront another young person with the good news. But the question always comes: How do we get started?

How to Organize for Visiting

1. *Begin with those persons who are most ready.* There's always some key young person who is sensitive to the big idea of helping others to find Christ. Begin with him. Work with him personally to get others interested. Maybe you're cooperating with others in a community-wide or denominational program. By moving ahead with others, some of your slow-moving folks may catch up. Perhaps some visiting young people from another church can help your group get the big idea. Let the idea catch fire—person to person. There's no other way. Pray about it. Take plenty of time.

Enlist your workers personally. Assume every young person is going to take part in this all-out effort to win others.

2. *Call together your key youth and adults.* As soon as possible bring all the youth in your church in on your planning. Your general planning committee should include every officer—youth and adults— and every teacher. Start planning several months in advance of the dates for your youth evangelistic mission.

Call some special business sessions of your senior and older youth to get the idea before them.

3. *Work through committees.* Your young people and your adult counselors must take the initiative for reaching the youth of your community. You'll need a planning committee to make your over-all plans. They may assign short-term committees of one or two persons for specific responsibilities. Always work through all your Sunday-school classes and youth groups in the church. Don't overlook anyone. Work together.

You may find it easier and more efficient to work through your planning committee, then let your subcommittees grow out of the needs of the group. Maybe a committee of one can handle some of your responsibilities. These are the committees you'll need:

Planning Committee	Publicity Committee
Visitation Committee	Worship Committee
Prayer Committee	Transportation Committee
Fellowship Committee	Finance Committee

Begin with visitation. You'll need a visitation committee to enlist your youth visitors, draw up your list of prospects, assign your teams, and plan your coaching sessions.

Second, there are your prayer services. Assign responsibility to some person for organizing prayer groups and around-the-clock prayer vigils. You may want to arrange for a prayer for youth in each service of worship. Begin at least a month in advance.

Third, plan for your fellowship times. Your fellowship committee will plan for your meals at the church. You'll need some parents to help here. Plan how you're going to bring your new members into your group.

Fourth, publicize your services. Get out posters. Write letters. Plan for newspaper stories and pictures. Get your story before the community with radio and television. And remember, your best promotion is person to person.

Fifth, you may need a worship committee or perhaps a music committee. Do you need a choir and ushers? You do if you are planning

57

for special services. Will you have a rally or a speaker as a part of your evangelistic effort? Get out some invitational "reserved seat" tickets. Plan big.

Sixth, of course somebody is going to have to line up some cars for transportation. You'll need to get your visitation teams around. You will be asking your families to sacrifice their family cars for the weekend.

And finally, there are always finances. How are you going to raise your money? From your budget? From an offering? You'll have meals and materials to pay for. You'll want to assign definite responsibility to someone to approve your bills and see that they're paid.

Don't just name your committees and forget them. See that they do their job. Keep them moving. Make witnessing every Christian's job.

One pastor says, "If they won't work, we put them on our prospect list and go see them!"

4. *Schedule your preparatory steps.* Make a big wall calendar. Use it as a check list of local church preparation, step by step.

Begin three months in advance; check these items:

You'll want to begin enlisting your youth visitors. Are your young people finding prospects? Are your prayer groups at work? Is your publicity moving? Are you making a study of the motives and methods of evangelism? Are you making efforts to reach your inactive young people?

Two weeks in advance of your date, check these items:

Complete your prospect lists. Are your cars lined up for all your teams? Have you personally enlisted your visitors for the stated times they will call? Do you have a telephone network set up to every member? Do you have plans all set for an around-the-clock prayer vigil ahead of your mission? How about your cottage prayer groups in the homes? Are your prayer cells moving ahead spiritually?

One week in advance of your endeavor, check these items:

You'll want to begin your intensive training of all your workers. Include every active young person. Arrange assignments by age groups. Make a master list of your prospects. Let your teams select whom they'll go with and whom they'll visit. You may need to devote an entire Sunday morning and evening to preparation.

5. *Plan your weekend.* Lay out a step-by-step, hour-by-hour schedule for your youth evangelism program. The heart of the youth-to-youth visitation plan used by most local churches is a weekend devoted entirely to youth evangelism. Sometimes a number of churches may work together, simultaneously. Often guest young people and their adult leaders come in to help and to learn. But the only place where a youth mission to youth can function is the home church.

Make up your own schedule. But be sure to include at least three or four periods of visitation. Here's a suggested schedule you may use as your guide:

Friday evening

> 4:00 P.M. Briefing session. Team your visitors and make assignments.
> 5:00 P.M. "Why should we visit?" Brief devotional talk by a youth
> 6:00 P.M. Fellowship supper
> 7:00 P.M. First visitation period
> 9:00 P.M. Report and sharing of experiences
> 10:00 P.M. Prayer circle and benediction

Saturday morning

> 8:30 A.M. Breakfast at the church
> 9:00 A.M. Briefing session
> 9:30 A.M. Second visitation period
> 12:00 NOON Lunch at the church. Reports and sharing

Saturday afternoon

> 1:30 P.M. Briefing session
> 2:00 P.M. Third visitation period
> 4:00 P.M. Reports and sharing

Saturday evening

> 6:00 P.M. Fellowship banquet

Sunday morning

    9:30 A.M. Sunday school. Welcome your newcomers.

    11:00 A.M. Morning worship. Youth emphasis and participation

Sunday afternoon

    12:30 P.M. Buffet luncheon for youth visitors

    1:00 P.M. Briefing session

    2:00 P.M. Fourth visitation period. Visit your "call-backs" and "not-at-homes."

    4:00 P.M. Reports and sharing. Free time

Sunday evening

    6:00 P.M. Fellowship supper. New members, special guests

    7:00 P.M. Dedication service

6. *Adapt the schedule to meet your needs.* For instance, you may visit the early part of the week—say on Tuesday, Wednesday, and Thursday—and perhaps one evening after school. Or you may begin your visitation on Thursday. If you're cooperating with other churches, plan some of your meetings together, such as an opening session and a closing youth rally in a central church. Or you may combine your visitation with a series of evangelistic services, youth activities week, spiritual life retreat, youth revival, or Impact!

7. *Give a special name to your project.* Where churches work together in a community-wide interdenominational effort, you may want to use the name "United Christian Youth Mission" or simply "Youth Week." Some youth groups call their project "Youth Witness Week," or "Teen Witness Crusade," or "Christian Witness Mission," or "Youth Evangelism Weekend," or use the name, "Impact!"

8. *Ask for help.* Many times your denominational youth director serving the churches in your community can provide guest leadership. Often gospel teams or fellowship teams can come out to help you. Sometimes college students may be able to come to your church on weekends. The best help you can get for this work is someone who has had some experience.

Here's another place your denominational people can help you.

Chances are, you'll find loads of information and help if you write for it and go after it.

How to Plan for Impact!

There is growing evidence that visitation evangelism alone is not enough to get through to young people with the facts and the power of the gospel. The outreach of youth-to-youth visitation evangelism is indispensable in reaching the outsider. But many new forms of witnessing are needed if the quality of our existing fellowships are to help youth understand what it means to "answer God's call to be the Christian community."

"Impact!" is the key to a dynamic new emphasis in youth evangelism now underway as a major thrust of The Methodist Church. For those churches which are not content with visitation alone as a special concentrated effort, Impact! offers an action-packed and intensive strategy for involving many persons in planning, preparation, and implementation. It offers a concerted effort which climaxes in a week long effort, usually involving a cluster of churches working together.

Bill Peckham of the Methodist Board of Evangelism staff, who directs this program says: "We are suffering from inertia. We need a new way to help young people feel the impact of the gospel. So we conceived the idea of Impact! We have three goals for the program: to commit young people to be the Christian community; to give them the opportunity to share their faith with young people outside the Christian community, and thus to fulfill the Christian commission." [2]

This is an attempt at total evangelism through an intensive program that involves many persons in the church—adults and youth—in a united effort that may involve churches of an entire community, district, conference, or state working together.

The striking and simple name Impact! [3] is a neutral name that arouses the interest of both the outsider and the insider. The " ! " does for Impact! what it does for *Oklahoma!* The Impact! name on lapel buttons, posters, bumper stickers, and promotional materials provides an effective conversation piece. "What does *that* mean?" Everybody wants to know.

Impact! requires an adult worker with considerable skill and rapport with young people in each local church or cluster of churches. Such an adult leader serves as a catalyst to stimulate, inspire, and bring creative tension to bear upon local leaders to prepare and follow through in committees, prayer breakfasts, sacrificial luncheons, depth Bible study groups, and the use of creative audio-visuals.

A flexible committee structure of task groups, with functional short-term subcommittees working together, takes responsibility for all-over planning. For more than a month in advance small groups meet in regular prayer breakfasts and Bible study groups.

The week of intensive effort opens with a takeoff on the familiar "Come-as-you-are-party," disguised as CAYAP Day for "Come-as-you-are-participation."

Teen talks during the week, sometimes planned as sacrificial luncheons, are no-holds-barred sessions in which the adult leader guides the teen-agers in discussions about the problems facing Christian young people.

"During the first couple of teen talks, the questions center on drinking, sex, and other problems of social nature," Bill Peckham says. "But by Wednesday the young people are asking, 'What does it mean to be a Christian?' There is progress in their thinking. Their experiences begin to show the effect of Impact!"

At the sacrificial luncheons the young people pay the price of a full meal, but eat only a simple lunch. The money contributed is given to a selected mission enterprise, such as a camp for underprivileged children.

"This is our reason for sacrifice," Bill Peckham says. "We do not want to have an impact only on our own group. When we truly experience Impact! our hearts are broken and we know compassion."

A midweek get-together for a hootenanny, picnic, or planned recreation attracts young people and provides a welcome change of pace.

The guest leader-evangelist serves as a resource person, discussion leader, and preacher for the evening worship services during the week.

A final commitment service brings the week to a climax. The follow-up to the mission is entrusted to small groups of persons organized as "ICTHUS" (Greek for Jesus Christ) or the "Twelve," meet weekly for prayer study and who continue to seek ways to serve and to reach out to the outsider.

How to Prepare Your People for Penetration

Whatever plan or strategy you develop for penetrating the high school community with the gospel, you will need to prepare your people as carefully as though you were going into guerrilla warfare. If you send them out without proper equipment and adequate briefing, they'll get murdered, or wounded, or so shaken up from the encounter that you'll never get them back again.

1. *Assemble your tools for the task.* No soldier would go into battle without equipment. Look at it this way: an investment in youth evangelism pays dividends for two generations. You are recruiting future Christian laymen, homemakers, teachers, missionaries, and preachers. There is no investment you can make that promises to bring back so great returns for so little.

Experiment with your own materials. Try new and creative approaches to meet the needs as you discover them in your community. But remember it takes time and trouble to develop printed resources. Ask yourself, "Would it be better to spend this time working with people?" Resources prepared by your denomination are usually less expensive. Often they're more attractive than material you'll print yourself.

Here is where your own youth and evangelism people will help you. Write your denominational youth or evangelism headquarters for a list of recommended resources.[4]

2. *Train your workers in advance.* See that the resources are in hand in plenty of time and that your co-workers do their homework. Plan for as many preliminary planning sessions as people will be willing to give. Encourage the entire youth group to plan for a special elective study of the motives and methods of contemporary evangelism.[5]

Do some serious study in the morning sessions with the entire youth division on the theological basis for the work of Christian evangelism.[6]

Let some of the evangelistic audio-visuals help you. You will find an increasing number of films, filmstrips, and charts that will help to arouse a sense of awareness and concern for persons.[7] Check the notes in the back of this book.

Remember: The two greatest blocks to effective evangelism are a lack of time and a lack of depth. Allow for extra time through prayer a chance to work by providing a supportive climate of expectancy. Guerrilla soldiers need a home base for basic training, morale building, and renewal. The church can be that home base. But our mission is in the world.

3. *Plan for on-the-job training.* Evangelism is a do-it-yourself movement. There's no other way. But we have a maintenance task in building morale, receiving reports, keeping persons moving and growing.

You will need some on-the-spot briefing sessions for latecomers. Plan to review the "Guidelines for Reaching Minds and Hearts." The next two chapters on "How to Reach Minds and Hearts" and "When You Talk with Others" will give you some resources to use for the training of *your* twelve.

SOME THINGS TO DO

1. Make up a wall calendar of achievement and plans for your youth group.
2. Make an exhibit of youth evangelistic resources available.
3. Outline a program of training for youth visitors in your church.

As the Father has sent me, even so I send you.
　　　　　　　　　　　　　　　　—JOHN 20:21

7

HOW TO REACH MINDS AND HEARTS

*Monologue is the language of the one who claims to have the answers.
Dialogue is the language of those who have been broken open and know
they are the ones being questioned.*

　　　　　　　　　　　　　　　　—LOREN HALVORSON[1]

How can we do a better job of reaching the minds and hearts of
others with the gospel? Of course, the first thing is to be prepared ourselves—to know what the gospel-in-relationship means.[2]

Evangelistic encounter is the doctrine of the Incarnation in action.
Christian conversation is the impact of life-upon-life—the personaliza-
tion of love. So when you are doing the work of an evangelist—sharing
the Christ you know with others—you are transforming love into
action, giving the gospel hands, feet, and lips.

Our best opportunities to witness to others open up at times and
places when we least expect it. But most of us do not take the time to
get involved deeply with persons and to talk to them about faith and
life and our relationships to the church. Visitation evangelism writes
witnessing into our schedule. Planned person-to-person evangelism
thrusts a name in our hands and on our hearts. Planned visitation com-

pels us to take the time to try purposefully to reach others for Christ.

Dialogue can take place only between two people. As soon as a third person steps in, however close and intimate he may be, the tone of the conversation becomes less personal. So you may decide to try one-to-one visitation evangelism. Or you may want another person to go along, either to learn or to reinforce and strengthen the impact.

Let's assume now you have your assignment. You are ready to go out and visit. You know this person casually, but not intimately. He's a name and a face, but not a person. You are at his door. Now as you ring, you're praying, "Nobody home—I hope, I hope." But somebody is home. And there *you* are. And there *he* is. What do you *do?* What do you *say?* What will *he* do? What will *he* say?

Guidelines for Reaching Minds and Hearts

1. *Open up.* You hear footsteps at the door. And here he is—your first candidate for discipleship. How do you open up? Well, put yourself in his place. When anybody comes to your door, what do you want to know? You have two questions: "Who are you?" and "What are you doing?"

Maybe you know him. He might even be looking for you. Perhaps you have written him a letter. Do everything in the first few minutes to create an easy, open situation. Do what comes naturally when young folks get together. Set the family at ease. Remember the introductions. You will want to pay respect to certain people by calling their names first. Stick to this rule and the rest will be easy. You pay respect to a woman, always; and an adult before a young person; a girl before a boy; the person you are with, when introducing one friend to another. Keep introductions casual and friendly.

Then in the first minute *tell why you've come.* You might say in your introduction: "We're visiting every young person we know who we feel ought to be in our church and youth fellowship. Of course we wanted to come to see you."

Get the other person's attention in these first few moments. A team of girls in Indianapolis called on one young man before breakfast.

He popped his head out of an upstairs window to see what they wanted. "Get dressed and come down here! This is important," they said.

A few minutes later they had a new recruit and a new visitor. He went out to help them call on others.

2. *Give yourself.* When you share your deepest ideas and feelings with another person, he is motivated to respond in the same way. Therefore giving of yourself results in getting deeper and richer communication with the other person. The best way to get another person's attention is to give him yours. Someone once said, "The best thing you can bring to a friend's home is yourself." When you stand on his doorstep you are saying, "I care about you."

He may be surprised you came to see him. Often a boy will say, "I'll call my mother."

And you will say, "No, we didn't come to see your mother."

"My Father, maybe?"

"No, we came to see you." This is enough to arouse his interest and attention.

I have a friend who sometimes moves in on a gang of beachcombers in an effort to infiltrate the group with the gospel. He is a kind of a nobody to them, at first. He makes himself known, gradually wins their friendship. He lives with these people, wearing only a swim suit for days at a time. They accept him as a person. He brings Christ into the conversation anonymously. "I have a great friend I wish you knew," he will say. Then he begins to describe all of the fine qualities of character of the living Christ, telling them who he is.

Try this yourself. How does your relationship to your greatest friend sound when you put it into words? Your own statements will set the tone of the conversation. People tend to open up about as much as we are willing to open up ourselves. If we put on a mask and keep ourselves hidden, others will follow our leads.

Try to get into the habit of expressing your ideas and feelings openly —within the bounds of discretion. Of course, you won't tell everything you think and feel. But we are much too secretive by habit rather than by necessity. A baby is charming and lovable because it is just what it is. If it is happy, it laughs. If it is angry, it cries. But by the time we are in our teens we are carrying on our interpersonal relationships as though the less the other person knows about us, the better. Of course everyone needs intimacy and privacy. But often we climb inside our disguise and nobody ever sees who we really are. Christian conversation in depth calls for openness and honesty and trust.

When the other person talks about his school, you might mention something about yours. When he talks about his interest in sports or music or fiction, you might express your preference. But you can lead out, too, in bringing your own attitudes and interests to the fore. Indeed, he will expect you to, because you have taken the initiative in coming to see him. You must have a reason. Why are you here? What do you really think? What do you live by? Give him your real self. It's your best gift.

We can say: "This is the way life looks to me. . . . What do you think?"

3. *Draw out.* Not many of us come right out with what we really mean when we start talking. We tend to begin with impersonal statements, conventional efforts to get acquainted, relieve silence, or to help get going. Introductions are like this. Finding a time and a place to talk is one way to draw out. "Do you have time to talk with us tonight, or should we come back?"

If the TV is on you might sit it out. When the TV or radio distracts you could ask: "Is this a favorite program?" If so, offer to come back. Perhaps you can talk in another room. The other person has to make some effort to meet you half way.

A real breakthrough comes when the other person brings a problem out into the open. Of course, we can deal with problems superficially as *outside* our realm of reality. It's like the student in a fraternity bull session who said to another: "Say that again so I can argue with you." No encounter here!

Real personal confrontation in conversation comes when we are involved, when we take a risk: "Can you tell me just what Jesus Christ means in your life?"

Sometimes silence will draw a person out. We can just continue to look at him, give him our attention, and wait. This will let him know that we want to hear more.

If he won't talk, say what you think. Maybe this will stimulate him to talk. Keep asking: "What do you think?"

4. *Ask questions.* To draw out, ask questions that require the other person to give some structure to his answers rather than just "yes" or "no."

To get a conversation moving or to loosen up a silent tongue, try these two surefire springboards:

"Tell me about . . ." and "What do you think of . . . ?"

Some types of questions can be a barrier. There's the detective question: "Why don't you go to church?"

There's the probing question: "I have a feeling you're holding something back . . . ?"

Or there's the inquiring question that asks for information. Nothing threatening about this: "Were you reared in the church?"

Try for questions that bring out essential thoughts or feelings about a person's faith and life. Ask questions that will stir his conscience; help you to understand each other; get his problems and objections and hopes and feelings out where you can deal with them together: "Have you ever thought about what your participation in our youth fellowship could mean to you?" Or: "Tell me how you feel about—" Take your clue from what you know about your common interests and where you feel that your interests and the Christian fellowship meet his.

Ask questions. What kind of questions? Well, if you merely talk about church membership or joining your youth fellowship, the person you ask can tell you, "No, I don't want to join." And that's the end of that. But if you make your appeal on the basis of religious involvement, you have a chance of getting through to people. "What has your faith meant to you?" "At what points do you feel the church has let you down?" "How have we failed you?"

5. *Listen carefully*. Jesus often began his parables by saying "Listen!" Again and again he clinched his point by saying. "He who has ears to hear, let him hear!" Yet how much of our lives we spend in poor listening. We must learn to give our total attention to the other person and hear him out. Only as we listen will he hear us. "Monologue" means "one word." Dialogue is listening to what is happening to the other person. Sometimes we sit impatiently waiting for the other person to get through so we can talk.

Be a careful listener. It is more important to understand this person than it is to "sign him up." You may get his signature and not get him. Really listening to another person means putting yourself inside the other person's shoes, knowing how he feels.

As a person talks, you will discover his ideas, his convictions, his attitudes, his problems, his feelings. Encourage persons to express their feelings freely. Persons can be themselves without pretense only when we receive them as they are.

Healing and redemption depend much more on what others say about themselves than upon what we say to them. And we must be the kind of persons that people feel they can talk to. Can they count on us to listen to them? Get rid of the idea that conversation means constant chatter. Any time that you feel you must talk just to fill the silence, you are very likely to call attention to the awkwardness of the situation. Silence can bring creative tension to bear on conversation—if we have the patience to listen and wait.

6. *Interpret back*. If your question calls for an explanatory answer, and you still get a meager answer, probe further. Ask him to tell you more. Or repeat in a questioning tone, part of what he says: "Did I hear you say . . . ?"

When the other person says something that is unclear or which can be interpreted in several ways, say what you think he means and offer this to him. Frame in your own words what he seems to be thinking and then ask—"Is this what you are saying—?"

Say what you think he says and see if he agrees with you. If he accepts your statement, you have understood what he means. If he doesn't, you have to try again.

The sure-fire way to test your understanding and to show that you are listening and to make sure you both are on board, is to say: "Let me see if I understand what you are saying—"

This attitude is such an important key to interpreting back that I want to repeat this for emphasis: *"Let me see if I understand what you are saying—"*

When we interpret back we are saying to the other person: "I want to understand. What you are saying is important to me."

7. *Avoid blocks.* It's easy to set up barriers to communication. Here are a few of these blunders that short-circuit the flow of dialogue:

First, *never interrupt.* This is a cardinal rule in drawing out. If you interrupt, you frustrate the other person's effort to talk and he may stop trying altogether. Furthermore, you imply that you're more interested in your own thoughts than his. So he may not feel like competing for your attention.

Second, *don't encourage a conflicting conversation.* If somebody starts another conversation, give a brief courteous reply then turn your attention and his to the main channel of communication. Try to keep out opposing static.

Third, *don't argue.* When we argue with another person, no matter what we say or how we say it, what the other person hears is: "I'll set you straight," or, "Let me talk. I'll tell you how this is—" If a person says something with which you don't agree, hear him out. Listen to him. Draw him out. Make sure you understand. Interpret back. Restate his objections. When you restate what he says, you show him you are listening. He feels that you are trying to understand. You have accepted his feelings, though you may not agree. You have no right to disagree until you hear him out. Then you can say, "Yes, I think I see, but do you see . . . ?"

Fourth, *don't reassure.* When a person poses a problem, our first impulse is to reassure him. Don't. When we reassure another person our ultrasonic message always says: "Don't be too concerned." "You're doing all right." "Live on the surface of life." Draw him out. Encourage him to express his feelings. Support him by getting into his struggle with him. Hear him out first. Then speak.

8. *Respond to feelings.* Somehow we get the idea that it's wrong to have feelings or to express them. Yet each of us has deep feelings about the things that matter most. How we feel about ourselves, about others, about our faith is more important than what we think. So if we respond to ideas and problems and ignore feelings we are in trouble. In any discussion a current of feeling flows along the same channel as the words. It is the feeling that gives power to the words.

As persons talk, they may express anger, anxiety, guilt, loneliness, embarrassment, joy, or hope. These expressions of feeling are woven into the fabric of the conversation. Sometimes emotions are so subtle that we can't distinguish feelings from the threads of ideas. To reach hearts we must respond to these feelings in two ways: by showing acceptance and sympathy. Here's how to respond helpfully:

First, *show acceptance.* To relate meaningfully to another person you must let him know that you are aware of his feelings and that you accept what he is saying. You must respond to him in a way that does not make him wish that he had kept his true feelings hidden: "That hurts, doesn't it?" "You feel deeply about that, don't you?" "I can see why you feel this way."

Second, *show sympathy.* Perhaps a better word is "empathy." You establish rapport ("fellow feeling") when you express appreciation of the other person's feeling. Empathy has nothing to do with whether or not he is justified in his feelings. You are merely expressing sympathy. And sympathy sparks communication. He doesn't want logic. He just wants someone to accept what he is saying and to sympathize with him. After you show you understand his feelings, you can say most anything you feel is appropriate. "Yes, I see. But do you see?"

9. *Let him decide.* Follow his leads. Watch for his greatest moment of sensitivity and insight. If you find that dialogue is taking place in an atmosphere of love and assurance and understanding, you will find that

there is another inner dialogue with God that is going on too. You can't make up another person's mind for him. But here's something you can do: *You can stir his mind and open up his heart so that the Holy Spirit has a chance.*

This inner motivation of the still small voice speaking to both of us provides the power that liberates, awakens, and reveals the persons we may become.

When such moments of decision come, we are at a turning point—a crossroads where life may take a new direction. Our life thereafter will depend upon acting upon such moments. It is at this point that we may say: "You feel, then, that you'd be interested in giving the Christian way a try?"

Sometimes a commitment card may serve as a "conversation piece." Conversation about the card may help to define the commitment a person may make. Read each affirmation on the card carefully together, point by point. Ask questions: "How do you feel about this? What do you think?"

You may ask: "If you feel this meets your needs and helps you to affirm your faith, you may wish to record your commitment. What do you think?"

Take your time. Don't exert pressure. The question is: Are you willing to begin where you are, take what faith you have, and let God direct your life?

10. *Depend on God.* Do your best. Never give up. Don't get discouraged. This is God's work, and he is at work too. While we are speaking to one another, he is speaking to us too. As we carry on an audible and spoken dialogue, his Holy Spirit is speaking to the inner man. As we commit ourselves to one another in conversation, God himself is here, too, giving himself to us in communion. As Dr. Paul Tournier says, "Compelling us to commit ourselves too." [3]

This experience of communion, community, and commitment is the experience of the presence, which is so central in the New Testament: "For where two or three are gathered in my name, there am I in the midst of them." (Matt. 18:20.)

Often the best thing that young people do in their calling is to pray. A team of two boys in Savannah were witnessing in the home of an unchurched teen-ager. As they were about to go, one of the callers said, "Would you like to join us in praying the Lord's Prayer?"

"I have never heard the Lord's Prayer," the boy said sadly, "but if you will pray, I will be glad to listen."

You might pray this prayer: "Our Father, we thank thee that a new disciple has just said 'Yes' to the Master's call—"

After you conclude your visit, leave. You may say, "This has been a great experience for us. We want to thank you for this visit."

SUMMARY

These ten Guidelines for Reaching Minds and Hearts are so important to the work of the evangelist that I want to repeat and outline them for emphasis. Memorize them. Practice them. Remember them. They will help you develop skills and create a climate in which you can introduce others to Christ:

1. *Open up.*
2. *Give yourself.*
3. *Draw out.*
4. *Ask questions.*
5. *Listen carefully.*
6. *Interpret back.*
7. *Avoid blocks.*
8. *Respond to feelings.*
9. *Let him decide.*
10. *Depend on God.*

Let no one despise your youth.—I Tim. 4:12

8

WHEN YOU TALK WITH OTHERS

I'm afraid the "do-it-yourself" movement has gone too far when a fellow who doesn't know anything about Evangelism is expected to do evangelistic work!

—Ralph Holdeman[1]

Maybe you're thinking: "This witnessing sounds good on paper. But I just can't do it. I wouldn't know what to do or say." Or this: "How can I talk to others about commitment to Christ? How can I share the deep things of the spirit?"

If this is what you're thinking, don't worry about it. The truth is, as a young person you have an entrance which not even your pastor has into the thoughts and minds of other young persons. You have a wonderful opportunity to witness.

But it is not enough simply to have an incentive to witness. You need to have some insights about how to approach people in personal conversation. You need some skills in human relations and personal work. How do you learn those skills?

How do we learn anything? Well, we have been listening and reading about how we can reach minds and hearts from what others have found out about communication. Now we are going to take a look at how others do it in a dramatization. Then we will try some role-playing. After that, we should be ready for the task of attempting to talk to others about their Christian life and faith. As we consider this drama of witnessing and later try role-playing, recheck what we are seeing and doing against the ten guidelines for reaching minds and hearts in chapter seven.

We Learn Through Dramatization

Dramatization is something like our rehearsal of a play. We try out our role first. We project ourselves into a situation that may be like one we will face later in dealing face to face with a real-life situation.

Remember a doctor serves his apprenticeship as an intern before he begins to operate on real people.

How does a teacher learn to teach? First she studies and reads about teaching; then she observes another teacher teaching; then she practice teaches; then she is on her own.

Here's where the newer education comes in. We can begin to read and learn all we can about evangelism from the experience of others. Then we can see how others witness. We can learn through dramatizing and role playing. Dramatization helps us to step into another person's shoes. We can try out our new ideas and insights in Christian witnessing in advance of the real-life situation. Play-acting gives us a chance to learn without having to make our mistakes on real people.

A Drama of Witnessing

Let's begin our study of personal witnessing with the use of drama. Here's a dramatized story of a couple of young persons calling. John and Mary are obviously skilled in personal relations.

Try assigning roles and reading your parts. You may want to give the lines from memory. Later you may have an opportunity to present this scene on radio or television—as a dramatic production.

John and Mary are calling on Joe. They are at Joe's door now. We hear John praying:

76

JOHN: O Lord, open our minds and hearts so that you can speak through us what you want Joe to know and do. And help Joe to respond and begin the new life tonight. Amen.

Doorbell. Joe answers the door. He is ill at ease. He isn't sure why they are here.

JOHN: Hiya, Joe!

JOE: Hello, John!

JOHN: We are making some friendly calls for the church. You know Mary, I believe?

JOE: Hello, Mary. Of course! Come on in—both of you! *Joe closes the door.* I suppose you two are out raising money for the church, huh?

MARY: Better than that, Joe!

JOE: What's better than money?

JOHN: We didn't come for money at all. We've come for you!

JOE: Me? What do you want with me?

MARY: You see, Joe, we're members of the oldest Fishermen's Club in the world. You remember Jesus said: "Follow me, and I will make you fishers of men."

JOE: Evangelists, huh?

JOHN: Yes, Joe, but we are maintaining our amateur standing. We're fishing for the fun of it! This is Christian Witness Week at our church.

JOE: Yeah? Well, won't you sit down?

MARY: All the young people in our church are out visiting those we would like to have in our church and youth fellowship. That's why we've come to see you.

JOHN: Next Sunday is membership Sunday in our youth fellowship. A new bunch are coming in. The pastor is starting a membership class.

MARY: We wanted to have the chance to invite you.

JOHN: You are a candidate for membership, aren't you, Joe? Wouldn't you like to think about this?

JOE: You've got the right dope, all right. I've never belonged to any church; used to go some when I was a kid—before we moved here.

But I might as well tell you—I just don't intend to be pushed into this thing at all. I'm not interested in joining the church.

JOHN: We can see how you feel, Joe. You don't want to be high-pressured, do you? I'd resent that, too. We have no intention of asking you to do something you don't feel in your heart. We think you ought to have the chance to tell us why you don't go to church.

MARY: That's right, Joe. We're not going to try to talk you into taking any step you aren't ready for.

JOE: Well, this is a new approach! What kind of evangelists are you, anyway? You're out to get church members, and you're not going to talk them into it?

MARY: We're not that kind of evangelists, Joe. We're your friends. We're amateurs—you know the Latin word *amo:* "to love"! We love this!

JOHN: You can't talk anybody into a decision as important as this one is!

JOE: Well, I'll tell you how it is with me. I've seen some of these church folks who pretend to be so Simon Pure getting away with murder, secretly. I don't know your church kids here so very well; but in Springfield, where I came from, some of the guys who were big wheels in the church on Sunday cheated on their tests, and the teachers thought they were little angels!

JOHN: Let me see what you're saying now. You mean you think so much of the church that it shocks you to find people who don't live up to what they profess?

JOE: Yeah, I guess that's it. There's just a lot of guys who are phoney; it's all surface; no one has caught up with them.

JOHN: And you think they ought to be just as good inside as they profess to be outside. Is that it?

JOE: Well, they ought to try anyhow. I can't see that the church helps some people.

JOHN: You're all for what the church stands for, aren't you, Joe? You just don't see that the church and the youth fellowship help people to live up to Christ's standards. Is that it?

JOE: Yeah, I'm for what the church teaches, but I don't see that it would help me to go to church every Sunday.

JOHN: Then your question is whether or not you can find something in the Christian faith that will help you live up to what you believe in your heart?

JOE: Yeah, that's right. I might as well tell you: before I moved here, I got mixed up with the wrong crowd. We broke into the school. Tore up the place. Three of them got caught; they spent the night in jail; I got away; they had to go to juvenile court. I was just as mixed up in the deal as they were; I didn't know what to do. I knew they wouldn't squeal. I got panicky. I went to a preacher in town; he gave me a lecture. Made me feel pretty cheap. He was no help. I just had to work it out myself, best way I could.

MARY: You feel the church let you down? This preacher—

JOHN: Maybe you feel that you asked for bread and got a stone.

JOE: Huh! What's that?

JOHN: That's something Jesus said. He said that God is like a good father. He knows how to give good gifts to his children. When a son asks for bread, he doesn't substitute a stone; when fish is on the menu, he doesn't serve scorpions!

MARY: John's preaching now, Joe! *Laughing.* What he's saying is this: We agree that you got a raw deal.

JOHN: Well, we know how you feel. We came here to give our witness. I guess maybe you've given us a better idea of what a redemptive fellowship really ought to be!

JOE: I suppose not all preachers are like that. And I think *you* understand what it means to be Christian—suppose I wanted to know more about your church; what should I do?

JOHN: Doesn't that depend on whether you're ready in your own mind and heart? That's the big thing, Joe.

JOE: I'd like to give it a try.

JOHN: Let me ask you, Joe—do you think you can affirm in your own heart: "I accept Jesus Christ as my Savior and Lord and will

79

try to follow his way"? If you feel this in your heart, you have already taken the first step.

JOE: Well, I think I've believed in Christ and the Christian way, but I haven't done much about it.

JOHN: You'd like to act on your conviction, then, wouldn't you, Joe?

JOE: Sounds all right to me. Count me in.

MARY: In moments like this we feel the need of prayer. Joe, would you join us in the Lord's Prayer?

JOE: Why, yes, of course.

ALL: Our Father which art in heaven, Hallowed be thy name. Thy kingdom come. Thy will be done in earth, as it is in heaven. Give us this day our daily bread. And forgive us our debts, as we forgive our debtors. And lead us not into temptation, but deliver us from evil: For thine is the kingdom, and the power, and the glory, for ever. Amen.

JOHN: Since you do accept Jesus Christ, you may want to make a record of your commitment. Here's a pen—you can make your record in duplicate so you'll have a copy.

JOE: You and Mary are pretty good fishermen, after all. *Laughing.* Let's see—this part about the youth fellowship—

MARY: We'll have our consecration service and reception of members Sunday night, Joe. Maybe we could come by for you. Couldn't we, John?

JOHN: Sure thing, if Joe—

JOE: That'd be fine. Say, I'm sure glad you came. This means a lot to me—I don't know when I've felt this way—this is—well, I'll see you Sunday. So long.

Evaluate What You've Learned

Now, let's stop and evaluate this experience.

In one evangelistic call these young people win a top-notch high school student who has been unfriendly toward the church.

How did it happen? What clues do we have? List your own points on the blackboard. Then discuss them. What made this visit by John and Mary effective?

Now, let's put down a few guideposts on our blackboard:

1. *John and Mary depend on prayer.* They pray before they call. They bring Joe into their prayer circle in the home by asking him to join them in prayer.

2. *They develop a friendly relationship.* They joke about their role as evangelists; they take Joe's crack about finances in stride. John and Mary let Joe know they are not going to bring pressure. Theirs is a low-pressure evangelism. They relax and enjoy themselves.

3. *They help to clarify the situation.* The visitors let Joe take the lead; they mirror back his thoughts. They try to understand Joe's position. They help Joe to see how he really feels.

4. *They don't argue with Joe.* John and Mary accept Joe. They help him along—one step at a time. Joe sees that they are interested in him, not in winning an argument or even in winning a convert they can report.

5. *The decision is Joe's.* The evangelistic visitors are ready to help Joe express his commitment—to make it articulate—even to get it in writing; but they put the emphasis upon *Christian experience:* "If you feel this in your heart, you have already taken the first step."

6. *They make their own witness unobtrusively.* "Yes, Joe, we are maintaining our amateur standing. We're fishing for the fun of it!"

7. *They compliment Joe.* John says, "I guess maybe you've given us a better idea of what a redemptive fellowship really ought to be."

Here are young people in a person-to-person encounter, helping others to find Christ. Barriers come down, and at the right moment Christ is there as the third person on their team.

How to Tackle Your Problems by Role Playing

One reason our moral and spiritual education is not more effective is this: We try to push on to our objectives by talking about them rather than showing young people how to work them out. Talking and preaching about right action doesn't do the job with adolescents.

They have to be shown, and they need to learn for themselves through experience.

Role-playing is an effective technique for helping your entire group take part in the solving of problems that arise in visitation evangelism. The purpose of role playing is to make a situation, idea, or problem seem real. The situation then becomes easier for you to understand and discuss.

You need to understand that there's no easy way to meet many of the situations and attitudes you'll find in these person-to-person relationships. Role playing is not a magic formula. It's a method that takes in your entire group. Take time to discuss and share in a stimulating process. Act out your problem. Think and work through to a number of solutions to the problem or to the best possible solution.

One caution: Don't use role-playing to parody a situation. No need to show folks what *not* to do. The effective unrehearsed drama searches for a real solution to a real problem people are facing in their lives.

Here are the steps in the use of role playing as a discussion stimulator and problem-solving guide:

1. *Select your problem*. Let suggestions come from your group. List them on a blackboard. Choose the typical problem that they're most interested in. It should be a real problem. Let it grow out of actual experiences. Make it realistic.

For instance, here is a parent we'll call Dave McNott. Dave seems to be interested in having his boy, Bill, go to church. But Dave McNott is not a committed Christian himself. However, Dave does all the talking for Bill, answers all your questions. Bill seems interested. But he doesn't have the background to understand the Christian faith, the Christian ethic, or the Christian fellowship. His dad dominates the situation. Bill hesitates to speak for himself. The visitors have difficulty in getting through. What should they say or do? It is a common and typical problem. (Of course you won't use real names.)

2. *Set your stage*. Let your group work out a specific real-life situation illustrating the problem. Decide how many people you need to

act out the roles. Two visitors, the mother and father, and the boy, five in all, should be your maximum number. Let the group set the stage. Talk through the part of the interview you will dramatize. What are the attitudes and personalities of the cast? What are the chief objectives of the interview? What difficulties will you run into? What outcome will you seek? What commitment should your visitors try for in this case?

3. *Assign observers for each role.* Suppose your group is large. Ask them to divide themselves into groups of five. Assign a member of the buzz group to each actor in the drama. Do this early in the game. Then your observation teams may assist in the selection of your cast. They may help define the problems and attitudes held by your various role players.

4. *Enact the situation.* Five or ten minutes are enough. Let the drama go on until the basic trend of the interview works out. Let the actors clearly establish the relationships and probable outcomes for your group.

Assign specific names—other than the real names of the actors—to each player. Encourage each person to express the attitudes which the group assigns to each stand-in.

5. *Get the reactions of your cast.* Let each person tell how he feels being in the other person's shoes. Encourage players to throw themselves into their parts. One of the greatest values of this play-acting is that it permits you to take on "empathy" with another person. Acting out assists you to understand how others feel. It helps show forth why they act as they do. You get a deepened sensitivity and insight into the problem. You search out valuable points of departure for the discussion that follows.

6. *Get the reactions of your observers.* Ask for observations and questions. Try these questions:

What points did the actors handle well?
What mistakes or omissions did they make?
What suggestions for improving the action do you have?
What would be the probable long-range outcome of their action?

Christian witnessing is not easy. Learning to guide young people in their attitudes and decisions is a skill that requires sensitivity.

So if you are a friendly counselor attempting to guide persons into a meaningful Christian experience, remember this: The golden rule is the best possible guide for dealing with others. *Treat the other fellow as if he were you.*

Witnessing Must Be Done with Our Lives

We've seen how others witness in the dramatization we've used here. And we've been doing some shadowboxing through our role playing. Now it's time to get out and begin to work and witness with real people. We've listened and read; we've seen what others are doing. But we really haven't learned about witness bearing until we begin to practice what we've learned. Youth-to-youth evangelism is a do-it-yourself movement. The purpose of all this is that one young person may tell another young person about Christ.

When you put yourself in the other person's place, you have a fellow feeling for him. You can say honestly, "This is the way you feel, isn't it?" You understand the other person—and this is what evangelism is all about.

When you first try to win another person to Christ, you're likely to say, "I'm going to win out," or "I'm going to lose out." Don't go with this attitude.

You need to say, "I'm going to break through to understand this person." It's better to understand a person than it is for you to "sign him up." For if you don't understand him, you won't "sign him up" anyway—not really. You may get his signature, but you won't get him. Try to "break through."

Well, you've rehearsed your role as a witness for Christ. Do you feel as if you're ready to tackle a real life situation? A real person? A friend? That's the test of the integrity of our witness.

As Harry Denman says, "We must do more than proclaim the gospel with our lips. It must be done as Jesus did it—with our lives."

SOME THINGS TO DO

1. Select your cast. Develop the drama of witnessing with John, Mary, and Joe. Present it to your group for a special program.

2. Arrange to present your drama on your local radio or television station as a part of a youth broadcast.

3. Write up a case study of some person and some problem you know. Ask your group to tackle the problem through role playing.

I have called you friends.

—JOHN 15:15

9

IF THEY'RE WORTH GETTING, THEY'RE WORTH KEEPING

Youth organizations, because of their interesting activities and attractive friendships, have an appeal to those outside the church. If real Christianity can be found within such a group, everything the members do to bring in others is evangelism. —LUCY M. ELDRIDGE[1]

Suppose you put out a lot of effort finding the young people you weren't reaching. You get your young people to go out and bring the outsiders in. Some young people are coming to your church for the first time. Many have already professed Christ. What happens to them now?

Do they stick?

Remember, we have just two jobs in the church: disciple winning and disciple developing. How do we develop these new disciples now that we've got them?

We are sure of this: *If they're worth getting, they're worth keeping.* Fortunately we know more about the skills of winning and developing young people in the Christian life than we have ever known before. Christian education is making great strides in this direction. Christian evangelism, too, is giving a great deal of attention to developing disciples. These skills are yours for the doing.

To help you remember them, I'm going to call these suggestions:

Twelve Ways That Work to Develop Disciples

Mine is not an exhaustive list. There are dozens of ways for you to develop disciples. You'll think of many ideas yourself. But let's just take twelve ways that successful churches are using to develop new disciples:

1. *Help youth find a firm faith.* Everything we do in the youth program of the church should, of course, contribute to a young person's understanding of the Christian faith. Faith shapes our actions, determines our philosophy, gives meaning to our daily living. Our Christian faith is an experimental faith; we must express our faith in relationship to the problems we face in everyday living. Young people need to see how their Christian faith is related to such problems as: understanding the other sex, getting along with others, enjoying leisure time, developing Christian character and leadership, understanding their own behavior, getting along with their parents, and looking ahead to marriage.[2]

Our Christian faith begins with Jesus and ends with him. If we want to know what God is like, we look to Jesus. If we want to know what life is all about, we turn to Jesus. He is our Alpha and Omega. In our modern alphabet Jesus is the *A* to *Z* of our Christian faith.[3]

Our Christian faith centers in Jesus' life and teachings. If youth are to have a firm faith, they must meet the "author and finisher" of our faith—consistently, through study, through worship, through meaningful action.

You've gone out and said to youth, "Come be a disciple of Jesus." If they've going to make good on the decision they've made, they have to know who Jesus is and what he taught. That's why everybody who works in the youth program should share in the responsibility of developing a vital program of study and worship. Your challenge now is to live up to the expectations you've raised by your invitation to youth: "Commit your life to Christ and his way."

2. *Bring their parents into the picture.* Don't overlook their parents. They can influence their teen-agers to be faithful and active. Plan for a parent-youth night. Give parents a picture of the purpose of your youth fellowship program. Stress the value of Christian education in the lives of their children. Parents are your best asset. You may win the entire family to Christ through the teen-agers. You can make faith a family affair.

A pastor in suburban Chicago says, "We invited our parents to our closing commitment service. We now have their loyalty and cooperation as never before. They saw what we are doing for their boys and girls."

Parents often follow their children in their choice of a church. The youth may lead the entire family into a new way of life. In Des Moines, Iowa, a director of youth work overheard this conversation in a hamburger stand.

One man said to another: "These two boys called on Mike last night. They asked him to join the church. We didn't know Mike was interested. They got him into their youth group. Mike is going to join the church. He signed up for the pastor's class.

"Ethel and I talked it over last night after they left. We decided to go into the church with Mike. If it's good for Mike, it ought to be O.K. for us."

3. *Write them a letter.* I have a letter I prize written by a pastor in Indiana. Sam J. Cross was once my pastor. And I've conducted evangelistic missions for him. His influence is written across the lives of hundreds of people in parishes he has served.

When you read his letter, you'll see why. He wrote personally to each young person making a decision. I have his letter in front of me now as I write:

FIRST CHURCH
Our Town, Indiana

Mr. James Hoosier
Our Town, Indiana

Dear James:

This letter is just to tell you how glad we are that you have accepted Christ as your Saviour and have dedicated your life to his service. This is the most important step you have ever taken. As you stand true to your promise, your life from this time on will be filled with joy for yourself and helpfulness to others.

If you are already a member of church, your consecration to him will make you a better Christian. If you have not as yet joined the church, this step will make it easier for you to do so. Let nothing prevent you from becoming a member of the church of your choice. Fellowship with God's people in the church will be of a great help to you in living a Christian life.

Having made your dedication to Christ, as a result of our invitation, naturally we would be glad to have you become a member here. However, if you decide to unite with another church than ours, we pray God's blessings upon you there, that you may be the very best Christian it is possible for you to be. Those who are uniting with our church are to have the rite of baptism and be received into full membership on Palm Sunday, at the morning worship service.

Special sessions of the church school in the next few weeks will emphasize what it means to be a Christian. You will want to be in regular attendance at these worship and study times, morning and evening.

The members of our church and your teachers join most heartily in this message to you.

Your pastor,
Sam J. Cross

4. *Give them orientation and training.* The most effective way to keep new members is to make their training for church membership

and reception into the church a matter of great importance. Most pastors consider that a minimum of four membership training classes is necessary for teen-agers. If young people have not joined the church until their high school years, they should have an intensive course of preparation in membership before they are received into the church.

You'll want to begin with an introduction to regular private and family devotions. Encourage them in their habits of church attendance. Give them an opportunity to pledge to the church budget. Put in their hands a good devotional guide such as *Power* [4] or *The Upper Room.* [5]

Give your new converts a good religious book. One of the pocket-size youth books is good for this purpose.

You'll find excellent helps for new members in your denominational literature. [6] Many denominations have special manuals for teen-agers. One of the handiest helps for Methodists in membership training is G. Ernest Thomas' chart *Spiritual Life for Methodist Christians.* [7]

Here's how an Indiana pastor works it:

"I give all members in training personal instruction in their homes. I go into the home first for a spiritual guidance visit and to make arrangements for their personal instruction. I let them know about the four sessions for membership training I will have with them in their homes. Sometimes the family takes instruction all together. I visit each home personally once a week for four or five weeks. I give each new member personal instruction using this chart. I follow the plan of having four sessions: on beliefs, the Methodist heritage, the church at work, and the duties of a Christian. If a pastor will take this time and trouble with his new youth and adults, it will pay great dividends in discipleship."

5. *Plan for a meaningful reception of members.* The decision these new members make in the home should be confirmed in the church. Your denominational handbook for the youth fellowship will give you suggestions for your consecration service. This is a time for the re-

dedication of all members—new and old. You may want to plan for an altar time for prayer in the sanctuary or chapel in closing.

6. *Hold open house for your newcomers.*[8] Teen-agers have the habit of dropping around to the homes of their friends after school. You can make this habit work for you. Here's how: Plan for your get-together in one of the homes of your church youth. The girls plan for refreshments. You get the word around to all your newcomers at school. Your old-timers say, "We're dropping over to Martha's Thursday after school for cokes. Some of our kids from the church are getting together. We'd especially like to have you come too. I'd be glad to meet you after school. Where shall we meet?"

You see how your open house works? You have an opportunity to meet your newcomers on neutral ground. Your regular folks get to know them as persons. Your fellowship is on firm ground. You're saying, "We appreciate you as a person—not just as a member."

7. *Give them challenging tasks to do.* Find out about their interests and skills. A new Christian won't go very far without having a chance to express his experience through service.

Is June musical? Ask her to sing in the choir.

Does Joe like to write? Put him to work on your church paper.

Is Don concerned about social problems—segregation, world peace, alcoholism? Let him head a committee to study the problem and come up with a study and action project for your group to do.

Is Jack an extrovert? Maybe he'll make you a good officer for your group. A born leader.

Is John an introvert? Perhaps he's just the person to lead your prayer cell or Bible study group.

Is Dave handy with a paintbursh? How about refurbishing your youth room?

Their hobbies and interests are a real clue to the skills and vocational possibilities of your young people. Maybe you need to think in terms of a vocational clinic for your youth. Your denominational leaders can offer you supporting literature and suggestions.[9] Help your young people to see the work they are doing—right now—as a Christian calling. Their rehearsals for larger work to come ought to be taking place right now.

8. *Continue to follow through.*[10] You may not get the young people you are trying to reach on your first try. Then try again. Second and third visits are often more productive than first attempts.

The pastor of a Fort Wayne, Indiana, church says:

Our follow-through is bringing in more young people all the time. Our visitors were disappointed when some of the kids they invited to our youth banquet didn't show up. They called back. Even two and three times. Every week. Our call-backs really are getting results. Those we bring in the hard way are showing more interest after the first wave of enthusiasm than those who came on the first invitation. Our young people are eager to witness regularly now. They see what a difference it makes.

9. *Develop the buddy system.* You know how the buddy system works in swimming. When the whistle blows, every person grabs the hand of his buddy. Each one reaches one. If you lose your grip on your buddy, there's trouble. The search begins.

How does the buddy system work in your church? It's simple. Take for example a boy we'll call Andrew. Andrew wins Tom. It's Tom's first decision. Andrew sees that Tom gets to his first meeting. He says to the others, "I want you to know Tom."

He sees that Tom meets the pastor and the other adult counselors. Week after week Andrew stays by him. He helps him to get in a prayer cell group. He sees that Tom knows the others and feels at home. He sits with him in church. Andrew is Tom's sponsor when he joins the church. But Andrew doesn't confine his activities to Sunday school and church. He makes it a point to get to know Tom as a friend. He pals with him at school.

You see how it works. Andrew's assignment is on a secret pal, a big brother basis at first. Tom gets to know the group through Andrew. He is established in his Christian habits and church attendance. Now Andrew's relationship to Tom is on a less formal basis.

Sometimes this sponsor is called a "fellowship friend." He has a big job, an important assignment.

A boy-and-girl team may develop into a class of two in boy-girl relationships! It might be worth a try!

If they're worth getting, they're worth keeping!

10. *Organize your visiting on an ongoing basis.* I don't know of a single growing Protestant church in America that does not major in two-by-two visitation evangelism regularly.

Some of the small fry have junior-high chapters of the "Fishermen's Clubs." They are popular and effective. One group calls theirs "Young Anglers"—another, "Minnowmen's Club"!

The response of young people moves like a chain reaction. The attitude of one alert teen-ager is typical: "Daddy," she said, "why hasn't our church asked the young people to do something important before this?"

Witnessing is not something that happens only on a weekend of stepped-up activities. Evangelism is like keeping house and raising children. You have to keep at it.

The best way to keep your new member is to get him to win others. When a person finds Christ, he has an experience that he needs to share. If he doesn't share it, he may lose it.

Most churches set aside one night a month or one night a week for their Fishermen's Club. This keeps witnessing on people's schedules. And on their minds and hearts.

11. *Call them up.* Keep them tied to the church with a telephone line. Teens are good at that.

A church in Montana puts teens' telephone talk to good use. Let a Montana pastor tell you how they do it:

Here's the way it works: The committee gets on the phone—usually at the church. They may begin as early as 2:00 P.M. Sunday afternoon. Youth fellowship meets for 6:00 P.M. "dine-a-mite." They call every person. They tell each one about the meeting. They catch a lot of young people in an hour or two of calling. Different teams work each week. Each person gets a reminder. Attendance is at an all-time high.

93

Young people in a church on the main line in Philadelphia call their telephone network "tele-fishing."

12. *Don't get discouraged.* Witnessing is hard work. You won't always be successful. Not by a long shot. But don't worry about it. You don't have to be successful. You may be sure that God is more interested in his children than you are. Count on his help, his guidance. Give God a chance with young people.

Some of your babes in Christ may die stillborn; others may be neglected and die; others may be so malnourished that they never develop. Some children of God may remain forever children.

Jesus said, "Feed my lambs." That's our job.

Every new Christian needs what a doctor prescribed for a new baby. He wrote on his prescription pad "T.L.C."

"What's that?" the baby's father asked.

"That," said the doctor, "is *Tender Loving Care.*"

A puny baby can develop into a vigorous athlete with T.L.C.— *Tender Loving Care.*

"If they're worth getting, they're worth keeping."

And you shall be my witnesses.

—ACTS 1:8

10

EVERY CHRISTIAN AN EVANGELIST!

Jesus Christ is the gospel we proclaim. He is also Himself the Evangelist.
                                        —THE EVANSTON REPORT[1]

One big idea caught on with the people in the section on evangelism at the World Council of Churches meeting in Evanston in 1954.[2] It's the slogan that heads this chapter: "Every Christian an Evangelist!"

And the one technique which delegates from around the world agreed is the best way to get this idea across is a simple technique. What is it? These Christians from all churches agreed on one phrase to describe their technique: "Gossiping the Gospel." That's simple enough. Talk about it. Let the word become flesh—yours and mine!

This is the way Christ gets his work done in the world. Through people. The question is: "Do we really want to carry the gospel out into the world?"

Just suppose this idea "Every Christian an Evangelist!" really took hold of our generation.

The generation of young people that launched the Student Volunteer

Movement was obsessed with one idea: "The World for Christ in This Generation!" This missionary movement stirred the student world as few other movements have ever done. Thousands of young people volunteered to go overseas as missionaries. Thousands went out. Many of them are there today. The sincerity and depth of a young person's commitment was measured by his response to this call: "If Christ calls me to the mission field, will I be willing to go?"

If a young person faltered in answering this question, his Christian experience was suspect. His friends said, "Why aren't you willing to go as a missionary?" [3]

We are living in a different world today because of the missionary movement. Evangelism on a world scale was a new idea when these youth leaders took hold of it.

It's true that our concern with the youth in our churches is often motivated by our wistful hope that they will do better than we have done. The sober truth is, they should.

We are living in one of history's *kairos,* or climax times.[4] Great and crucial decisions are coming to sudden focus. These chaotic, unpredictable days have sharpened the struggle between the children of darkness and the children of light. We are finding in the attitudes of youth a climate that is far more favorable to the Christian faith than ever before. We are at the end of the age. And at the beginning of a new era.

> For each age is a dream that is dying,
> Or one that is coming to birth.[5]

The missionary movement among youth and students was a rehearsal for a larger evangelism in the church as a whole. The students who worked together in the missionary endeavor are the men who are the leaders in the ecumenical church around the world.

As a result of the missionary movement there is no "foreign" field now. The world is our parish. Step outside your door. You are in mission territory. The question young people are facing now is not merely: Will you be willing to go out to help save the world? The question is: Will you be a witness wherever you are? "In Jerusalem"—that's your home town—"and in all Judea"—that's your country—"and Samaria"—that's your neglected neighbor—"and to the end of the earth"—that's this mighty neighborhood that begins outside your door.

And there's a prior question: Will you help work for a world *worth saving?* One of the most thrilling chapters in the life of the church is being written by our young people. Youth are making a clear and challenging witness in a world of struggle. If the young people have their way, this may yet be the century that establishes human justice, realizes brotherhood among all men, and wipes war forever off the face of the earth.[6] For these are their concerns.

Let's just suppose that this idea "Every Christian an Evangelist!" is the wave of the future. Suppose we have in the youth evangelistic movement of our churches a preview of coming attractions in the Christian movement as a whole. What are the fruits of this newer evangelism?

Evangelism Brings Renewal to the Fellowship

There are some direct results of this newer evangelism and some indirect results, some immediate and some long-range accomplishments. The most direct results we can see right off.

1. *First of all, witnessing brings new faces into our fellowship.* And with a larger group our Christian fellowship has a large opportunity. Sometimes the new and reawakened interest of young people in the program of the church is phenomenal. In our western regional youth mission in Denver, attendance in the participating churches jumped 100 percent in many local youth groups overnight.

2. *Witnessing provides motivation for a better program.* Their awakened interest sparks everything the young people are doing. Witnessing improves the program. Young people say, "If we're going to invite others, we must provide a better program." The planning process takes on new importance. For young people see that worship

and study are their way of helping to make known the way of Christ.

3. *Witnessing brings new life to the group.* Witnessing often works where nothing else seems to breathe the breath of life into youth work. Youth in churches without organized youth work respond to the challenge to win youth to Christ. A pastor of a parish in Oklahoma says: "The churches in our county had been without an organized youth program for ten years. We got hold of this idea of witnessing. We rounded up the interested young people, studied what we needed to do to reach them, then went out and developed a parish youth fellowship of sixty young people. It has made our church come alive."

4. *Witnessing improves the moral tone of a community, too.* From a director of Christian Education in South Dakota:

We started our year with an average attendance of fifteen to twenty young people attending our evening youth fellowship. By the end of our school term eighty-nine young people had joined our group. Our Christian witness outreach brought them in. Now our youth teams visit our unchurched and inactive young people regularly one night a month.

A number of the young people we've brought in are outstanding. Some have made commitments to full-time Christian vocations.

Beer parties were prevalent in the high school last year. Now they've gone out of fashion. Our youth leaders in our church have become leaders in our school. Our football captain is our witness chairman. He takes every opportunity to share his Christian convictions with others.

Our young people now have a new concern for people. They drive as far as 350 miles to help small, out-of-the-way churches. One night they drove their car 100 extra miles to pick up four more football players after their game. Our group is bursting with enthusiasm and plans now. And our evangelism was the spark!

5. *Witnessing opens the door for service.* Look at any local church where the idea of a witnessing fellowship has come alive, and you'll find young people bursting out of the routine into creative service for others.

Take the movement in church extension, for example. The spiritual and numerical growth of the youth program in Florida has been fantastic. The key: a continuous emphasis on youth-to-youth evangelism. The young people who pioneered in these endeavors in youth evangelism a few years ago are now young adults. They have formed volunteer commando teams. They specialize in organizing charter members for new churches. The score to date: four new congregations in greater Tampa alone—an average of seven new churches a year for the state.

In Wichita young people have laid the groundwork that has made possible four entirely new churches in four years.

Youthful evangelists enjoy their work. A group of young people started a new church in Moses Lake, Washington, in a temporary home —a funeral parlor. One of them hung a sign on the door: "You'll be here some day. Why not Sunday? Charter services at 11:00 A.M. Come and worship."

6. *Witnessing brings a new understanding of the redemptive fellowship*. Out of the give and take of these times together comes a new sense of fellowship. Young people carry on their creative work in witnessing in the style and atmosphere of a summer work camp. Youth often live together in a central church. They work together, worship together, and witness together. By studying and worshiping and serving they gain a new understanding of the redemptive fellowship.

Phil Ritter, youth secretary for the World Council of Churches, tells this story of the redemptive fellowship: "One summer recently young people from America and a number of European countries came together for a work camp in Austria. One of the girls from Czechoslovakia, a girl we'll call Marie, saw her parents and older brothers liquidated during the Nazi occupation. One night after our day's work, our group of students began talking about building Christian fellowship. Marie said, '*Build* Christian fellowship? We can't *build* Christian fellowship! We *celebrate* Christian fellowship!"

Yes, out of their experience of witnessing comes an understanding of the nature of the Christian fellowship—the redemptive fellowship.

Evangelism Strengthens the Christian Faith

The indirect and inner results of witness bearing are harder to put your finger on. Yet the testimony of every young person who witnesses to his faith in Christ is always, "I got more out of this than the persons to whom I witnessed."

1. *Evangelism evangelizes the evangelist!* A Rocky Mountain, Montana, college student writes of her experience helping in our Denver mission: "If I never live another day, I can feel that once in my life I helped make Christ vital in lives that may have always been blind to his way. It has given me an urge to do something, and that I will."

2. *Then, too, witnessing makes prayer real.* Prayer is a strange and baffling experience for many young people. Witnessing gives point and purpose to their prayers. They see their prayers for others answered— sometimes almost before their eyes.

Two boys in Savannah called on a fellow who claimed to be an agnostic. The boy said: "I don't believe there is a God, and if there is, I don't care." The boys took the challenge. They stayed with him for an hour. They laid bare the faith that was in them. They found beneath the boy's crust of indifference a heart that was hungry. They witnessed. They prayed. As they left, the boy said, "This is the first time —" and he couldn't finish.

3. *Christian witnessing has a way of clarifying the choice of a full-time Christian vocation.* Young people have a chance to give the ministry a trial run. And they may make their choice of Christian service on the basis of experience on the job in serving as part-time shepherds of souls.

Our youth who bear witness learn from firsthand experience what it means to be born anew. They see the Christ and the church at work in the lives of people. They find that God's spirit is working through them. Often their witness goes far beyond what they have intended or expected. In a rural mission in Dade County, Georgia, two of our boys visited the father of a young man who had entered the ministry. Through one of those encounters that is hard to understand, these youthful evangelists were able to enlist the father for the Christian life and faith. The boys said humbly, "We were grateful for the sake of the son that the father came to Christ."

These boys are now themselves ministerial candidates. You can see the place evangelism will have in their ministry.

4. *Witnessing brings the experience of hearts strangely warmed.* The Christ of the Emmaus Road is walking along the American road too. Now and again he catches step with his youthful disciples. And they feel their hearts burn within them as he walks with them by the way.

I can never forget one of our first ventures in Christian witness with young people. I can see it now.

We are in San Antonio at the Texas Military Institute. We are in our final evening of a three-day youth spiritual life retreat during our Christmas holidays. Our young people are coming in from their first visits in nearby homes. They tell us about their evangelistic visits. They have been working with a clean-up list our pastor has given them. But they haven't known that. They report favorable responses in one home after another. And we learn for the first time that young people can "do the work of an evangelist." It is a historic moment. Their faces are so warm, so eager.

This evening, our last night together, we are observing Benedictine silence. (Were you ever voluntarily silent from dinnertime to breakfast the following morning? Talk about discipline—it's a soul-searching experience!)

The silence is too much for one of our girls, a girl we'll call Constance. We are sitting with some of the others in silence. Suddenly Constance blurts out to C. A. Greenwaldt, our director, "Tell me, C. A. do we really believe this?"

"Believe what?"

"This business about eternal life and the soul living forever."

We can see C. A. is overwhelmed for a moment. The question has come out of the blue. He seems to be thinking, "How can I marshall the evidence for eternal life?" But before he can get the words out of his mouth, he is interrupted. The headmaster of the school, J. D. Miller,

101

comes into the room. We are sitting just outside the door of his apartment. He doesn't realize we are observing voluntary silence this evening. He says, "C. A., I don't believe you ever met my daughter Allene. She isn't here with us now. But I have something she wrote. Wrote it last fall for her Latin class. The teacher gave the class a choice of subjects. For some reason Allene wrote this. The teacher asked Allene to read her theme before the class. She calls it 'Dust to Dust.' I'd like you to hear it."

The father reads what Allene wrote. The theme is one that any pastor would gladly bring for his Easter message to his people.

When he finishes, Miller says, "It's interesting that Allene wrote this. For within the year an encephalitis epidemic struck. Allene was one of the first to go."

Miller can say no more. Words aren't necessary now. A silent communion too deep for words settles down upon our group. Allene is speaking through her father to Constance—and to us—who are waiting in silence outside her door.

And through this silence I can hear another generation ahead taking up in a glad chorus what is only a whisper now: "Every Christian an Evangelist!"

NOTES

1

1. *The Christian Century,* September 30, 1964.

2. Edgar Z. Friedenberg, *The Vanishing Adolescent* (Boston: Beacon Press, 1959).

3. Excerpts from *Saturday Evening Post,* December 30, 1961, p. 63, "Youth: The Cool Generation." Gallup Poll Staff.

4. See *Youth are Laymen Too!* Pamphlet 2552–B for a fuller statement of the youth as laity. Division of the Local Church, General Board of Education of The Methodist Church, P. O. Box 871, Nashville, Tennessee 37202.

2

1. The resources for small groups in mission are growing and are good. Some of the best:

Robert A. Raines, *New Life in the Church* (New York: Harper & Row, 1961). Adult orientated. A study of what one church has done in revitalizing the lay ministry.

G. Byron Deshler, *The Power of the Personal Group*. Tidings, 1963. 1908 Grand Avenue, Nashville, Tennessee 37203. Deals in depth with trust, openness, and the climate for small groups.

Samuel Emerick, ed., *Spiritual Renewal for Methodism*. Methodist Evangelistic Materials, 1958. Nashville, Tennessee. A review of contemporary renewal through disciplined groups.

George Koehler, *The Evangelistic Encounter*. Division of the Local Church, General Board of Education of The Methodist Church, 1963. Box 871, Nashville, Tennessee 37202. Guidelines for training youth and adults in the work of evangelism in summer programs, spiritual life retreats, encounter conferences.

Reuel L. Howe, *The Miracle of Dialogue* (New York: Seabury Press, 1963).

So You Are Going to Join a Koinonia Group. United Presbyterian Church, Division of Evangelism.

Witness in Daily Life Groups, leaflet. Commission on Evangelism, 231 Madison Avenue, New York, N.Y. 10016.

The Twelve, handbook by Harold Rogers; *Tools for the Twelve*. Suggested materials: "The Twelve." Newsletter, 1908 Grand Avenue, Nashville, Tennessee 37203.

Christian Outreach, Box 115, Huntingdon Valley, Pennsylvania 19006. Resource materials for growth by groups; secular interest groups; Christian outreach.

2. From Ross Snyder, *Toward Nothingness or Existence*. One of the best guides to depth Bible study. The Board of Education of The Methodist Church, 1963. Box 871, Nashville, Tennessee 37202.

3

1. Dick Gilbert, *Winning Friends for Christ and the Church*. The Division of Evangelism, Board of National Missions, Presbyterian Church in the U.S.A.

2. Gerald J. Jud, *The Deed–The Word—in the World,* Division of Evangelism, United Church Board for Homeland Ministries, 287 Park Avenue, South, New York, New York 10010.

3. Ray L. Henthorne, *The Church's Educational Ministry: a Curriculum Plan* (St. Louis: The Bethany Press, 1965).

4. *The Objective of Christian Education for Senior High Young People*. Commission on General Christian Education of the National Council of Churches, 1958.

5. For a brief statement on the objectives, see *Becoming Christian,* 2414-C. Division of the Local Church, General Board of Education, The Methodist Church. Box 871, Nashville, Tennessee, 37202.

6. Shelia D. Woods, *Youth Ventures Toward a Vital Church* (Nashville: Abingdon Press, 1965). Provides resources for worship, discussion, and action. The final chapter provides addresses of voluntary service projects.

7. John D. Perry, Jr. *Coffee Houses: Evangelism or Evasion?* Order from Service Department, Box 871, Nashville, Tennessee 37202 or Tidings, 1908 Grand Avenue, Nashville, Tennessee 37203.

8. *Making Teen Centers Succeed.* The New York State Youth Commission, Albany, New York. Free Booklet.

9. Haskell M. Miller, *Understanding and Preventing Juvenile Delinquency* (Nashville: Abingdon Press, 1958). Practical resources for individuals, church, family, and community.

10. *Invest Your Summer.* Published annually by the Commission on Service Projects, 475 Riverside Drive, New York, New York 10027.

11. C. Frederick Stoeker, *Committed to Serve.* A manual to aid in developing local service projects. Ecumenical Voluntary Service Projects, Commission of National Student Christian Federation, 475 Riverside Drive, New York, New York 10027.

12. Lee E. Dirks, *Religion in Action.* The National Observer, Silver Springs, Maryland, 1965. A report in depth on how America's faiths are meeting new challenges.

4

1. Howard W. Ellis and Ted McEachern, *Reflections on Youth Evangelism. Youth Evangelism—New Reflections,* 2524-C, a set. Division of the Local Church, General Board of Education of The Methodist Church. Order from Service Department, Box 871, Nashville, Tennessee 37202.

Reflections on Youth Evangelism and the leader's guide, *Youth Evangelism —New Reflections,* are available only in the complete set.

2. Reuel L. Howe, *The Miracle of Dialogue,* p. 3.

5

1. Religious Census Packets are available from Tidings, Materials for Christian Evangelism, 1908 Grand Ave., Nashville, Tennessee 37203. Packets for 500 population, for 750 population, for 1,000 population, and so on.

2524–C, a set. Division of the Local Church, General Board of Education of The Methodist Church. Order from Service Department, Box 871, Nashville, Tennessee 37202.

Reflections on Youth Evangelism and the leader's guide, *Youth Evangelism —New Reflections,* are available only in the complete set.

2. "Doctrinal Foundations of Evangelism," *Shepherds* magazine, January, 1950, Nashville, Tennessee.

3. I am indebted to Wally Chappell for this interpretation of Christian fellowship and for many of the ideas found here in this chapter.

4. "Effective Witnessing," by Roy L. Smith, *The Christian Advocate,* September 13, 1956, p. 22.

5. *Becoming Christian,* 2414–C. Service Department, Division of the Local Church, General Board of Education, The Methodist Church. P. O. Box 871, Nashville, Tennessee, 37202.

6. See *How to Organize a Teen-Club,* The Nehi Corp., Columbus, Georgia.

From your library of fun and fellowship try these books:

Larry and Helen Eisenberg, *The Omnibus of Fun* (New York: Association Press, 1956).

E. O. Harbin, *The Fun Encyclopedia* (Nashville: Abingdon Press, 1940).

E. O. Harbin, *Gay Parties for All Occasions* (Nashville: Abingdon Press, 1950).

Larry and Helen Eisenberg, *The Pleasure Chest* (Nashville: Parthenon Press, 1949).

The federal government provides funds for Teen Posts for certain churches who will provide leadership and supervision as a part of the "Great Society" program.

You may be able to qualify. Check with your area coordinator for the War on Poverty Program for information.

6

1. Andrew W. Kurth, *Taking Others Along.* Michigan Christian Endeavor Union.

2. For information on Impact! write The Rev. Bill Peckham, the General Board of Evangelism, The Methodist Church, 1908 Grand Avenue, Nashville, Tennessee, 37203.

3. See ch. 4 "Why Should I Witness?" pages 37-43 for a development of the threefold theme of Impact! Commitment, community, and commission.

4. See your own denominational youth handbook and youth evangelism literature. You may have conference or synod or state headquarters and staff who can help you with resources, literature, and field service. Here is a list of action books in evangelism:

Robert F. Jones, *That Youth May Know* (Richmond, Virginia: John Knox Press).

Winning Friends for Christ and the Church. Manual for Youth Evangelism, Presbyterian Church in the U.S.A. Office of Youth Evangelism, 156 Fifth Avenue, New York, New York.

Forrest B. Fordham, *The Christian Witness*. B.Y.F. of the American Baptist Convention, 1951. Philadelphia, Pennsylvania.

For a current list of resources available from The Methodist Church, write for the free leaflet: *Resources for Evangelism in The Methodist Youth Fellowship,* 2367–B. Service Department, P.O. Box 871, Nashville, Tennessee 37202.

5. Howard W. Ellis, *The Witnessing Fellowship* (Nashville: Abingdon Press, 1961). An elective study for Senior Hi Youth. Four sessions and two dramatic skits for the prologue and epilogues.

6. Gordon Pratt Baker, *A Practical Theology for Christian Evangelism* (Nashville: Graded Press). Deals with the moral and spiritual responsibilities for evangelism in relation to the Christian doctrines of God, man, salvation, the Holy Spirit, and the church. *A Theological Reflection on the Work of Evangelism* may be ordered from Department of Studies in Evangelism, World Council of Churches, 475 Riverside Drive, New York, 10027. One of the most provocative of contemporary studies.

Peiter De Jong, *Evangelism and Contemporary Theology*. Tidings, 1962. Gordon Pratt Baker, ed., *Evangelism and Contemporary Issues*. Tidings, 1964.

John A. T. Robinson, *Honest to God* (Philadelphia: Westminster Press, 1963). This book is frankly disturbing—but it will make you think!

Hal and Jean Vermes, *Step by Step in Theology* (New York: Association Press, 1962). A programed instruction book adapted from Jack Finegan's *First Steps in Theology,* an experimental book for private study that works like a teaching machine.

7. Audio-visuals suitable for youth evangelism include: *Four to Go!* Sixteen mm sound film in black and white and color; 14 minutes. Tidings. Order from regional film library serving you. Synopsis: Three young people call on Marty, hoping to enlist her for witnessing for Christ. Marty backs off, pleads inexperience and a weekend trip. Her awakening comes when she meets a girl in distress on her trip. This leads to her concern for another. She urges

her friend Frank to join her in a call on this girl. When Marty realizes witnessing is simply trying to take Christ to those who need him, she becomes the fourth in *Four to Go!*

Members One of Another. Filmstrip; 59 frames, guide, and script. Deals with interpersonal relationships and sensitivity to feelings.

Conversion Plus. Sixteen mm. film in black and white or color; 38 minutes. Graded Press for the Editorial Division of the General Board of Evangelism by TRAFCO. The meaninglessness of life without Christ or the fellowship of the church.

It Makes a Difference. Thirty-five mm. sound filmstrip; 63 frames, color, 33 1/3 rpm record. (CDV) sale, postage.

7

1. Loren Halvorson, *Exodus Into the World* (Minneapolis: Augsburg Press, 1966).

2. Reuel Howe, *The Miracle of Dialogue.*

George Koehler, *The Evangelistic Encounter.* Division of the Local Church, General Board of Education of The Methodist Church, 1963. Box 871, Nashville, Tennessee 37202. Guidelines for training youth and adults in the work of evangelism.

3. Paul Tournier, *The Meaning of Persons* (New York: Harper & Row, 1957), p. 161.

8

1. *Who? Me?* The Board of Evangelism, Evangelical United Brethren Church, Dayton, Ohio.

9

1. *That All May Know* (New York: Friendship Press, 1947), p. 36.

2. See *How to Understand the Opposite Sex,* by William C. Menninger and others (New York: Sterling Publishing Co., 1956).

3. See ch. 1, "We Would See Jesus," *I Believe,* by Nevin C. Harner (Philadelphia: The Christian Education Press, 1950).

4. *Power,* devotional guide for young people. Box 871, Nashville, Tennessee 37202.

5. Daily devotional guide published by The Upper Room, 1908 Grand Avenue, Nashville, Tennessee 37203.

6. *Membership Manual of The Methodist Church for Teen-Agers,* by Leila Bagley Rumble (Nashville: The Methodist Publishing House, 1951).

7. Chart in four parts: (1) The Methodist Faith, (2) The Methodist Heritage, (3) The Church at Work, and (4) The Duties of a Christian. Tidings, 1908 Grand Avenue, Nashville, Tennessee 37203.

8. See *Winning Friends for Christ and the Church,* Manual for Youth Evangelism, The Division of Evangelism, The Presbyterian Church, 475 Riverside Drive, New York, New York 10027. An emphasis on evangelism through friendship. See also *Evangelism Through Friendship,* same address.

9. Write for *Resource Materials on Christian Vocations,* Service Department, Board of Education, Box 871, Nashville, Tennessee 37202.

10. Excellent audio-visual helps for youth-to-youth evangelism:

Gallery of Witnesses, one of the Youth Audio Visual Kit sound filmstrips. Write your publishing house.

The High Room, 20 min. color, guide. Producer: Southern Baptist Convention. Animated cartoon. Synopsis of the film:

  Story of "Cotton" Patch. Based on real high-school boy. The "High Room" is youth's upper prayer cell. Flash backs tell the story of boy's poverty, frustration, murder of his father in a labor dispute. Despite group's effort to include "Cotton," he remains aloof, unconvinced of their sincerity. Finally through other youth he discovers meaning of a redemptive fellowship and Christian experience.

10

1. (New York: Harper & Bros., 1955), p. 98.

2. For a popular easy-to-read report of the World Council of Churches meeting of 1954, see *Evanston Scrapbook,* by James W. Kennedy (Lebanon, Penn.: Sowers Printing Co., 1954).

3. See *Philosophy of the Christian World Mission,* by Edmond D. Soper (Nashville: Abingdon Press, 1943), p. 12.

4. See ch. 2, "The World We Face," in *The Whole Gospel for the Whole World,* by Alan Walker (Nashville: Abingdon Press, 1957).

5. From "The Music-Makers," by Arthur O'Shaughnessy.

6. See "Crucial Issues in the World Revolution," by Bishop G. Bromley Oxnam. *Motive,* November, 1955, p. 20.